German Jet Aces
of World War 2

D1289880

SERIES EDITOR: TONY HOLMES

OSPREY AIRCRAFT OF THE ACES • 17

German Jet Aces of World War 2

Hugh Morgan and John Weal

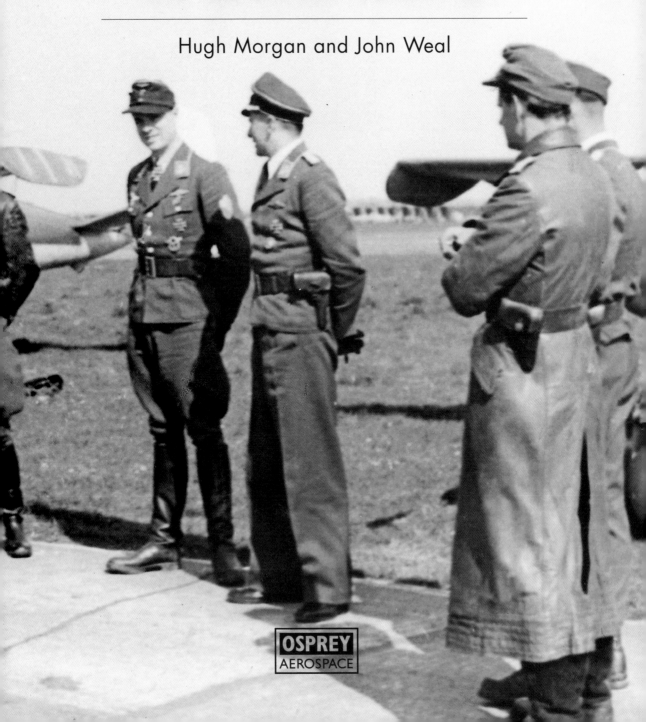

OSPREY AEROSPACE

Front cover
**Flying Me 262A-1a (Wk-Nr 110559)
'Red 13', III./EJG 2** *Gruppen-*
kommandeur **Oberstleutnant Heinz
Bär clinically disposes of a 387th
Bomb Group B-26B Marauder on 9
April 1945 – one of two Martin
bombers he was credited with on
this date. Within days of this action
taking place, Bär was posted away
from his** *Gruppe***'s Lechfeld base to
Munich-Riem, where he joined JV 44
(***cover artwork by Iain Wyllie***)**

First published in Great Britain in 1998
by Osprey Publishing, Elms Court, Chapel Way, Botley, Oxford, OX2 9LP

Reprinted Summer 1998
Reprinted 1999

ISBN 1 85532 634 5

Edited by Tony Holmes
Page design by TT Designs, T & S Truscott
Cover Artwork by Iain Wyllie
Aircraft Profiles by John Weal
Figure Artwork by Mike Chappell
Scale Drawings by Mark Styling

Printed in Hong Kong

EDITOR'S NOTE
To make this best-selling series as authoritative as possible, the editor would
be extremely interested in hearing from any individual who may have relevant
photographs, documentation or first-hand experiences relating to the elite
pilots, and their aircraft, of the various theatres of war. Any material used
will be fully credited to its original source. Please write to Tony Holmes at
1 Bradbourne Road, Sevenoaks, Kent, TN13 3PZ, Great Britain.

CONTENTS

HEINKEL v MESSERSCHMITT

When the sun rose over Mecklenburg on 27 August 1939, it held the promise of another glorious summer's day for the thousands of holidaymakers thronging that province's Baltic coast seaside resorts. But ten kilometres inland, along the banks of the River Warnow, it heralded an event of far greater import in the annals of aviation history – the dawn of the jet age.

There was hardly a breath of wind to rustle the low line of trees bordering the Heinkel works' airfield at Rostock-Marienehe as *Flugkapitän* Erich Warsitz settled himself into the cramped cockpit of the tiny aircraft sitting at the end of the single main runway. Early morning sunlight glinted off the bare metal panels of the machine's short fuselage and stubby elliptical wings as he quickly ran through one last instrument check. Watched by Ernst Heinkel and a small knot of mechanics, the aircraft began to roll. Gathering speed, it took to the air and swiftly (much more quickly than a conventional propeller-driven machine, or so it seemed to the excited onlookers) climbed to a height of 500 metres. Warsitz circled the airfield once and then came in for a perfect landing. In less than seven minutes it was all over.

Warsitz and Heinkel were carried shoulder-high back to the factory buildings where, despite the early hour, the latter lost no time in telephoning the Berlin apartment of Ernst Udet, the Chief of the Technical Office at the RLM (Reich's Air Ministry);

'Good morning', said Heinkel, 'I just wanted to inform you that *Flugkapitän* Warsitz has just successfully flown the world's first jet plane, the Heinkel He 178, and landed safely.'

The dawn of a new era in aviation. The Heinkel company led the field in early rocket and jet technology, as witness the illustrations on this and the next two pages. Although no authentic photograph is known to exist of the first aircraft in the world to fly solely with a liquid-fuelled rocket motor, this artists's impression gives a good idea of the shape and size of the diminutive four-metre span He 176. Note the semi-supine pilot's position in the extensively glazed nose

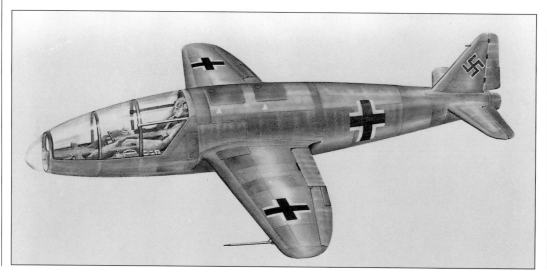

After a moment's pause Heinkel was rewarded with a few drowsy words of congratulation before Udet pointedly requested that he be allowed to get back to sleep. In fact, Warsitz had just pulled off a remarkable double. Currently 'on loan' to Heinkel, Erich Warsitz was chief pilot at the Peenemünde experimental rocket station. It was here, two months earlier, that he had also undertaken the maiden flight of the first aircraft in the world to be powered by a liquid-fuel rocket motor, the Heinkel He 176.

But the Luftwaffe hierarchy failed completely to recognise the significance of these events – and this despite (or perhaps because of?) the fact that war was only a matter of hours away. It might have been of some small consolation to Ernst Heinkel at the time had he known of the difficulties which Frank Whittle was even then experiencing in trying to persuade the powers-that-be in the RAF to take seriously *his* research into jet propulsion!

The He 178, a purely experimental design, was retained in Rostock for use as a testbed throughout much of the war. The almost equally historic He 176 fared less well. It was dismantled and sent to the Berlin air museum, where – still in its packing cases – it fell victim to a Bomber Command raid in 1944 which saw the destruction of much of the building and many of the exhibits it housed, including the giant 12-engined Dornier Do X flying-boat.

Undeterred, Ernst Heinkel continued his development work. This resulted in the He 280 twin-jet fighter, which made its first powered flight – of three minutes duration – on 30 March 1941 (some six weeks before Frank Whittle's turbojet finally got airborne on 15 May 1941 in the specially-built Gloster E.28/39). Six days after its maiden flight, the He 280 was demonstrated to Ernst Udet, now the Luftwaffe's *General-Luftzeugmeister* (Chief of Aircraft Procurement and Supply). Udet's initial enthusiasm for the Heinkel may have been tempered by the knowledge that a specification for a jet fighter had already been issued to the rival Messerschmitt company at Augsburg, in Bavaria.

Over the next two years the two manufacturers, Heinkel and

Just two months after the maiden flight of the He 176, test pilot Erich Warsitz achieved the double by taking to the air in the He 178, the world's first jet aircraft. Like its rocket-powered stablemate, however, the He 176 was a purely experimental machine . . .

Messerschmitt, vied with each other for an official production order. The He 280 was claimed to be faster and to possess a better rate of climb and a higher service ceiling. Weighing against it was the fact that it had only some two-thirds the range of the larger Messerschmitt design, that it was under-gunned and that the twin fin and rudder arrangement of the vertical tail surfaces was suspect. Other reasons 'of a technical nature' were also said to favour Messerschmitt's proposal, but these may have been politically motivated.

Whatever the truth, or otherwise, of such allegations, it fell to Erhard Milch, who had been appointed to the post of *General-Luftzeugmeister* after Udet's suicide in November 1941, to sound the death knell for the He 280 in a letter to the Rostock factory dated 27 March 1943;

'My dear Herr Heinkel,

'It is with regret that I have to inform you of my decision to delete the He 280 from the development programme in favour of the Me 262. As you yourself know, the overall war situation today no longer allows us to run two designs side by side. But I would request that you complete the prototypes up to and including the V9, as these are to be used as flying testbeds for the various turbojet engines currently under development.

'All other work on the design, particularly constructional and the finalising of blueprints, is to be discontinued. Furthermore, I would ask that you inform my department as to the nature and number of He 280 components beyond the V9 which have already been completed.

'I wish to express my most sincere appreciation for the work you have undertaken to date and for all the new knowledge gained about jet aircraft as a direct result of your initiative. I hope that the experience you have acquired will lead to the development of new designs in the future.

'I remain, with best wishes and Heil Hitler

'Your

'Milch.'

. . . and nearly two more years were to pass before Heinkel's – and the world's – first jet fighter design, the twin-engined He 280, was ready for flight. The three-minute hop on the afternoon of 30 March 1941, with test-pilot Fritz Schäfer at the controls, beat Britain's single-engined Gloster E.28/39 by a scant six weeks

The Me 262 referred to in the letter above had started life as the P.65, a proposal submitted by Messerschmitt to the RLM in the summer of 1939, just weeks before the maiden flight of the He 280. The first Me 262 to take to the air powered by jet propulsion alone did not fly until three years later when, on the morning of 18 July 1942, *Flugkapitän* Fritz Wendel lifted the third prototype (Me 262 V3) off the Leipheim runway for a flight lasting just twelve minutes.

It is perhaps indicative of the secrecy and intrigue which surrounded the Me 262 that Adolf Galland, who (in his position as *General der Jagdflieger*) was ultimately responsible for planning and directing future fighter operations, had not even known of its development until early in 1942. And even then he was kept in the dark as to its progress until he finally flew the fourth prototype on 22 May 1943. It was after this flight that Galland made his now famous, and oft-quoted, remark that piloting the Me 262 felt 'as if an angel were pushing'.

Indeed, so convinced was Galland of the Me 262's potential that he recommended production of the Bf 109 be halted to enable Messerschmitt to concentrate all-out on the new model. Later he urged that every fourth fighter produced should be a jet. Galland's enthusiasm helped sweep away some of the hesitancy and vacillation bedevilling the Me 262 project. Just 72 hours after Galland's first flight, Erhard Milch ordered the jet into series production. Milch now accepted Galland's radical suggestion that the revolutionary nature of the new jet fighter justified an accelerated development programme. The first 100 aircraft completed would immediately be issued to special test commandos whose job it would be to iron out all the inevitable 'bugs' in actual combat with the enemy. The practical experience thus gained could then be incorporated into subsequent production runs.

But one man did not agree with the *General der Jagdflieger*'s proposals. And in Nazi Germany that man's word was law.

Despite Heinkel's pioneering work, it was Messerschmitt who was awarded the contract to produce the Luftwaffe's first operational jet aircraft. Initial examples of the Me 262 were equipped with a tailwheel undercarriage. Here, test pilot Fritz Wendel lands the third prototype Me 262 V3 (PC+UC) after its first brief flight at Leipheim on 18 July 1942. The alarming cloud of smoke is caused by unburned fuel, which ignited in the tail of the port engine nacelle and poured onto the runway

One of the early Messerschmitt jet pilots was Feldwebel Heinz Herlitzius, seen here in studied pose – he was detached by the Luftwaffe to become a member of the Me 262 development team. A former EKdo *Thierfelder* pilot, he became the first man to exceed 1000 kmh when he put the Me 262 S2 into a power dive from 7000 metres on 25 June 1944. Herlitzius survived the conflict only to be killed in a car accident during the immediate postwar years

A staunch supporter of the Me 262 following his test flight of the fourth prototype on 22 May 1943, Generalleutnant Adolf Galland scored seven kills with the jet whilst serving as *Verbandsführer* of JV 44 in the spring of 1945

Adolf Hitler rejected out of hand the implementation of mass production and forbade any attempt at undue haste – 'Nothing will be done with the new fighter until *I* have decided on its merits'. He took his time deciding. And when it finally came, the decision condemned the entire Me 262 programme to continuing doubt and uncertainty.

The Führer was becoming increasingly obsessed with revenge and retribution. For him it was far more important to be able to strike back at the enemy than it was to provide his fighter arm with a machine capable of effectively defending the Reich against the increasing numbers of Allied bombers violating German airspace.

He had already decreed back in February 1943 that every new fighter produced should also be fully functional as a fighter-bomber. And when he led his entourage from his 'Wolf's Lair' HQ in East Prussia to nearby Insterburg airfield to witness a demonstration of the new fighter's capabilities in November of that year, the inevitable question arose: 'Can this aircraft carry bombs?' he suddenly asked Hermann Göring.

The Luftwaffe C-in-C, already primed by Messerschmitt, answered cautiously. 'In theory, yes, my Führer. There is sufficient power to spare to carry a 500-kg bomb-load, perhaps even 1000-kg'.

That was all the confirmation Hitler needed. 'For years I have been demanding a fast bomber from the Luftwaffe. And now, in this aircraft which you put on display to me as a fighter', he declared, 'I see the "Blitz Bomber". Of course, none of you thought of that!'

As far as Hitler was concerned, that settled the matter. He assumed that his wishes would be carried out and that the Me 262 would be modified for its new role of retaliatory 'Blitz Bomber'. In fact, nothing of the sort happened. Messerschmitt continued to develop his aircraft solely as a fighter. When the Führer learned of this some six months later he flew into one of his incandescent rages. This time, on 25 May 1944, he specifically *ordered* that the Me 262 be built as a bomber. It was only after a succession of high-ranking subordinates had pleaded with him to reverse this potentially disastrous decision that a single concession was wrung from Hitler – he would allow one Me 262 out of every twenty built to be completed as a fighter! Later, with the advent of the Arado Ar 234 (a true 'Blitz Bomber', designed as such from the outset), he relented still further. For every Arado delivered he would release an Me 262 to the fighter arm.

It was not until 4 November 1944 that Hitler finally gave permission for full production of the fighter version of the Me 262. But by then it was too late, for most of the Reich's major cities lay in ruins. Enemy fighters dominated Germany's skies and were drawn like magnets to the long, paved runways of those Luftwaffe airfields still intact and suitable for jet operations. Just getting the Me 262 into the air and down again became increasingly hazardous during the closing six months of the war. Many machines which, had they been available a full year earlier, could have cost the Allied air forces dear, were now destroyed on the ground, in assembly halls or while awaiting delivery to beleaguered and fuel-starved units.

One small part of Adolf Galland's ambitious proposals, however, had been implemented – the setting up of a test *Kommando* to operate the Me 262 under combat conditions.

KOMMANDOS, BOMBERS AND TRAINERS

On 9 December 1943 the *General der Jagdflieger* persuaded his superiors at the RLM to order the activation of an experimental jet fighter unit. Known as *Erprobungskommando* (Operational Test Detachment) *262*, it was to be based at Lechfeld, south of Messerschmitt's plant at Augsburg, in Bavaria, and had a planned establishment of 20 pilots. Command was entrusted to Hauptmann Werner Thierfelder, an experienced Bf 110 *Zerstörer* pilot, and latterly *Gruppenkommandeur* of III./ZG 26 (the assumption being that those with many hours of twin-engined operational flying behind them would find it easier to make the transition to the Me 262).

In the event, the detachment's first three pupils, who arrived in January 1944, were all from single-engined *Jagdgeschwader*, but they were hardly over-employed as EKdo 262 initially had just one jet. This was the fifth prototype (Me 262 V5), which was used almost exclusively by Thierfelder until he wrote if off in a crash-landing in February.

Gradually the situation began to improve. By the end of April the *Kommando* was operating two further Me 262 prototypes (including

This shot of an operational Me 262 (taken in June 1944) shows one of EKdo 262's complement of early production jets. This unit (sometimes known as EKdo *Thierfelder*) was composed of two *Staffeln* and one *Stab* unit, and its first aerial victory was scored by Lt Alfred Schreiber on 26 July 1944 when he shot down a Mosquito. EKdo 262's final victory also took the form of a Mosquito, destroyed this time by Lt Joachim Weber on 18 September, 1944. Just discernable in the background of this photograph is Me 262 V8 Wk-Nr 130003, which was one of the first jets to be fitted with armament. The premier jet taken on charge by EKdo 262 on 19 April 1944, V8 was destroyed in a landing accident the following October

One of the key Messerschmitt test pilots on the Me 262 programme was Gerd Lindner, who is seen here in casual dress alongside the more formally attired Hauptmann Werner Thierfelder – the latter was the first commander of pioneering Me 262 unit, EKdo 262, which formed in December 1943. Like Karl Baur (the chief test pilot specifically responsible for the Me 262 development), Lindner was especially valuable in the testing of armament systems for the aircraft

the V8, which was the first aircraft to be fully armed with four 30 mm MK 108 cannon), plus a few pre-production models. Early in May a dozen more pilots – six each from two of Thierfelder's old *Staffeln*, 8. and 9./ZG 26 – were posted in. Having only recently converted from the Bf 110 on to the Me 410, they now had to familiarise themselves literally from the ground up (the tricycle undercarriage was still very much an innovation in Germany) with another completely new aircraft.

Not only did they have to master jet handling and flight characteristics, the Me 262's high top speed – some 40 per cent faster than that of the Me 410 – and consequent wide radius of turn also meant rewriting the rule book on combat tactics.

Nor did the Me 262's innate superiority as a fighting machine automatically confer the same status upon the men assigned to fly it. And with no two-seat trainer version yet available, many found the transition hard to make. As one early trainee observed;

'Flying the Me 262 was a bit like the first few lessons when learning to drive a car. You knew where all the knobs and switches were. You knew what your hands and feet were supposed to be doing. There just wasn't the time to do it!'

One pupil ordered to take off and fly a circuit of the field on a later occasion found that, by the time he had retracted the wheels and flaps and adjusted the trim, the runway was no longer in sight! Although his plaintive excuse, 'This bird's just too quick for me!' did not go down well with his instructor (there were mutterings of disciplinary action for failure to carry out an order), it nevertheless became a catch-phrase among his fellow trainees.

As the war entered its final 12 months, the growing need to camouflage Luftwaffe airfields and installations presented ever-increasing problems for pupils desperately trying to locate the base that they had left from perhaps just minutes before. One unfortunate who failed to do so, despite twice flying the length of the runway and being assured by ground control on each occasion that he was directly overhead, finally elected to land at a smaller field he recognised nearby. He just managed to scrape in, juddering to a halt little more than 20 metres

from the perimeter fence. It took all his long-suffering instructor's skill to get the specially-lightened jet into the air again for the short hop back to base. Another quick-thinking tyro faced with bringing his Me 262 down on an airstrip of obviously inadequate length promptly let fly with his nose guns to add to the braking effect. Just what the effect on the resident personnel was of having a sudden salvo of 30 mm cannon shells whizzing about their ears is not recorded, but it's said the local flora and fauna was never the same again!

Despite such trials and tribulations Ekdo 262 was slowly beginning to turn out a trickle of qualified Me 262 fighter pilots. On 19 May 1944 the unit suffered its first casualty when Unteroffizier Kurt Flachs crashed the seventh prototype during a training flight. To make matters worse, a batch of reinforcement aircraft expected the following week failed to arrive. Hitler's unequivocal decree of 25 May that the Me 262 was to be a 'Blitz Bomber', and nothing else, was having its effect. Within 48 hours a chastened Göring had ordered that the control of all Me 262s be transferred to the *General der Kampfflieger*.

Somehow EKdo 262 managed to get around this edict. Although those ex-*Zerstörer* trainees who had not yet fully converted to the Me 262 were returned to their previous units, Thierfelder and eight of his pilots continued to quietly hone their fighter skills on the handful of machines which remained at their disposal, even after the full weight and focus of the jet programme had been redirected towards strengthening the bomber arm.

The first bomber unit selected for conversion to the Me 262 was *Kampfgeschwader* 51 'Edelweiss'. With the exception of Poland, KG 51 had fought in every major campaign of the war. By May 1944 the bulk of this highly experienced unit, also recently converted on to Me 410s (albeit the bomber version, rather than the *Zerstörer* variant operated by ZG 26), was stationed in France. On 23 May the *Geschwaderstab* and Major Heinz Unrau's I./KG 51 were withdrawn from their bases west of the Seine and ordered to Lechfeld for retraining on the Me 262.

This was easier said than done, for although it took only a stroke of the Führer's pen to transmogrify the Me 262 into a bomber, it would involve a lot of hard work before the first machine could take to the air

Me 262 V10 'VI+AE' (Wk-Nr 130005) was the first jet modified for fighter-bomber testing. Here, the V10 is being flown by Gerd Lindner, who is testing the *Deichselschlepp* towed-bomb concept. Maximum speed in this configuration reduced to just 325 mph. When the target was reached, the Me 262 was placed into a shallow dive, and employing the Revi gunsight, the pilot released the bomb by disengaging both the tow bar and wing simultaneously – not a successful innovation!

Pre-war Luftwaffe pilot 'Bombo' Schenck assumed command of the training programme designed to convert ex-*Kampfgeschwader* pilots onto the Me 262A-2a 'bomber' at Lager-Lechfeld on 20 June 1944

13

Me 262A-1a of EKdo 262 is seen at Lager-Lechfeld in the late summer of 1944. The man standing on the wing has been identified as Leutnant Fritz Müller, who later 'made ace' with JG 7. The aircraft itself, Leipheim-built Wk-Nr 170059, subsequently served with KG 51

as such. The first requirement was for an increase in range. This necessitated an additional fuel tank, which altered the aircraft's centre of gravity. The extra tank, plus the bomb load, made the bomber version of the Me 262 appreciably heavier (despite the reduction of the nose armament from four cannon to two), which in turn meant strengthening the undercarriage.

Initially, therefore, KG 51's conversion was restricted to the pilots of 3.*Staffel* under Major Wolfgang Schenk. For aircraft they took over EKdo 262's fighters, the majority of which had been hurriedly modified into fighter-bombers.

The Allied invasion of Normandy on 6 June 1944 added impetus to the training 'programme' which, for most pilots, consisted of just four or five familiarisation flights. The first Me 262 bombers were delivered at the beginning of July, the lack of bombsights in these early machines being a graphic indication of the haste with which they had been produced. It took a very experienced pilot to achieve satisfactory bombing results using just the standard Revi gunsight as an aid to aiming. This may have been a contributory factor to the Me 262's first service fatality when, on 14 July, Stabsfeldwebel Moosbacher crashed during a practice bombing run over the waters of the Ammersee.

By this time some dozen members of 3./KG 51 had been adjudged more or less proficient on the Me 262. It was standard Luftwaffe practice to name small independent detachments after their CO, and it was as the *'Einsatzkommando'* (Operational Detachment) *Schenk'* that nine Me 262s were scheduled to depart Lechfeld for France on 20 July 1944 – the very day of the now famous attempt on Hitler's life at his 'Wolf's Lair' HQ in East Prussia.

Only five made it to their destination, the airfield at Chateaudun, west of Orleans (two crashed on take-off, their pilots unaccustomed to the all-up weight of a fully laden operational Me 262, whilst another suffered a technical failure during an intermediate stop at Schwäbisch Hall and the fourth lost his bearings and made an emergency landing to the north of Paris). It was just eight weeks since Hitler had demanded that the Me 262 be employed solely as a 'Blitz Bomber'. But now, when his orders were on the point of being carried out, he effectively tied the hands of Schenk and his four remaining pilots with a ruling that, while over enemy-held territory, they were expressly forbidden to fly faster than 750 km/h and to dive below a height of 4000 metres!

It is little wonder that the *Eins.Kdo Schenk* made no impact at all on the fighting in the west (the Allies were apparently completely unaware of their presence; there being no mention of the Me 262 in any intelligence reports during the battle for France). Instead, the quintet of jets joined the general exodus, retiring via Creil and Juvincourt to Chièvres, south-west of Brussels. It was here, to the west of the Belgian capital on 28 August, that *Eins.Kdo Schenk* suffered its only combat loss when Oberfeldwebel Hyronimus Lauer crash-landed his machine to escape a flight of four P-47s from the 78th Fighter Group (FG) which had power-dived 'to within 50 metres of the slate-grey jet's tail'.

The unfortunate 'Ronny' Lauer would fall foul of P-47s again on 2 October. By that time, however, the *Eins.Kdo Schenk* had ceased to exist. On 5 September 1944 the unit was returned to the fold of 3.*Staffel*, rejoining a I./KG 51 now fully equipped with Me 262s and based at Rheine, in Westphalia. But Wolfgang Schenk was to retain his semi-autonomy for a few weeks longer. Throughout that September he headed a small two-aircraft detachment (somewhat grandiosely entitled the 'Kommando Edelweiss'), which was tasked with testing the new nose-mounted TSA (low-level and dive) bomb-aiming device.

While *Eins.Kdo Schenk* had been feverishly preparing for its ultimately fruitless foray into France, the other occupants of the Lechfeld complex, the handful of pilots of EKdo 262, had quietly – almost clan-

All the aircraft in this early EKdo 262 line-up at Lechfeld display the unit's distinctive mid-fuselage yellow band. The machine in the foreground, Wk-Nr 170071, is 'White 2', which was often flown by Major Erich Hohagen during his time with both III./EJG 2 and as *Kommandeur* of III./JG 7 (see colour profile number 8). The second aircraft, 'White 3' (Wk-Nr 170067), ended its days with KG(J) 54

The two photos on this page show 'White 10', an Me 262A-1a/*Jabo* (note bomb pylons under forward fuselage) of EKdo 262. The upper photograph illustrates well the slow shallow-climb technique of the jet during take-off – wheels quickly up, half flap and automatically extended leading-edge slots (see shadow thrown on the port nacelle). Note also the different style of tail swastika on Wk-Nr 170041 – one of a batch of Schwäbisch Hall-built machines – when compared with the previous illustrations. This aircraft later passed, via the *Kdo Nowotny*, to III./EJG 2

destinely – continued to refine and perfect their own brand of fighter tactics. But before these could be put into practice the unit suffered a heavy blow with the loss of their commander on 18 July.

There is some confusion as to the exact circumstances of Hauptmann Thierfelder's death. One German report maintains that he was killed in action against heavy bombers of the Fifteenth AF striking northwards into Bavaria from Italy, but there is no American evidence to substantiate this. Other sources state that he failed to return – for reasons unknown – from an anti-reconnaissance sortie. This latter theory is perhaps the more likely, as EKdo 262 initially concentrated its efforts on trying to intercept and bring down the RAF's high-flying Mosquito and Spitfire reconnaissance intruders.

On 26 July it was one such UK-based Mosquito, caught near Munich by Leutnant Alfred Schreiber, which was hailed as the unit's very first kill (although damaged, the Mosquito did, in fact, manage to reach the safety of an Allied-held airfield in Italy). Schreiber's second victory, a reconnaissance Spitfire claimed exactly a week later, remains uncorroborated. It may well therefore be that the first jet kill in history was the confirmed destruction of a No 540 Sqn Mosquito PR XVI –

another reconnaissance machine – shot down by Leutnant Joachim Weber over Ohlstadt, some 65 kilometres south-southwest of Munich, on the afternoon of 8 August. If, that is, one discounts the two pilot-less V1 flying-bombs destroyed by Gloster Meteor Mk Is of the RAF's No 616 Sqn some four days beforehand . . . the latter event itself a telling indictment of the 21-month German lead in jet development – the timespan between the maiden flights of the He 178 and the Gloster E.28/39 – frittered away by 'political' interference.

Seven days later, on 15 August, EKdo 262 downed its first, and only, heavy bomber – a lone B-17G reportedly flying along the Rhine shooting up river traffic as it went! A straggler from the 303rd BG, the Flying Fortress was eventually caught by Feldwebel Helmut Lennartz over the outskirts of Stuttgart. Fully occupied by the storm of flak being thrown up by the city's ground defences, the crew of the bomber apparently did not spot the jet bearing down on them.

'I scored hits on the left wing. The effect of my 30 mm shells was devastating. The wing was blown completely off', Lennartz later recounted. When he landed, the first person to congratulate the feldwebel was Professor Willy Messerschmitt himself.

By this time, perhaps detecting a slight lessening of Hitler's intransigence against the use of the Me 262 as a fighter, Adolf Galland was making plans to raise Ekdo 262's establishment to 40 aircraft. The unit, commanded since the loss of Thierfelder by Hauptmann Horst Geyer, an 18-kill *Experte* from JG 51, was to be divided into two Staffeln (built around cadres provided by the two original 8. and 9./ZG 26) under Oberleutnants Müller and Bley respectively.

Three days after his B-17 kill Lennartz, together with Joachim Weber (still the only two Me 262 pilots with confirmed victories to their credit), flew as Oberleutnant Müller's wingmen to Rechlin-Lärz. Although they had not been expected by the resident staff, the trio were assigned quarters in a deserted barracks on the southern edge of the sprawling experimental base. Here, they set up shop and prepared to receive the rest of the *Staffel*, the majority arriving by 21 August.

Being a test establishment, Rechlin lacked much of the equipment essential for the proper functioning of an 'operational' unit. The most glaring omission was an effective ground-radar control system. But this

A *Rotte* of Me 262A-1a/*Jabo* fighter-bombers of *Eins.Kdo Schenk* taking off from Juvincourt near Reims, where they were based for 48 hours during the long retreat from Normandy

was put right when the Signals Officer, Leutnant Viktor Preusker, requested permission to visit Berlin. There he found a complete Würzburg radar installation earmarked for the eastern front. With the connivance of some friends in high places, Preusker managed to have this written off as 'destroyed in a bombing raid' and quietly got it re-routed northwards to Rechlin!

Even with such initiative, the unit's brief deployment to Rechlin-Lärz did not meet with much success. The first missions were flown on 10 September 1944 but, as far as is known, only two victories were achieved – one on 14 September and the second four days later, both victims again being reconnaissance Mosquitos, claimed by Leutnant Joachim Weber.

Another, smaller detachment – the 'Kommando Wegmann', which was deployed to Erfurt-Bindersleben under the command of EKdo 262's adjutant, Oberleutnant Wegmann – fared even less well. Despite the benefit of a legally acquired Würzburg radar, it failed to claim a single kill.

It thus fell to those pilots of EKdo 262 remaining at Lechfeld (with sub-sections at Leipheim and Schwäbisch Hall) to score the lion's share of the victories during the final weeks of the unit's existence. Among those who claimed their first kills on the Me 262 during this period, and subsequently went on to become jet aces, were such luminaries as Oberfeldwebel Helmut Baudach from JG 2 'Richthofen', who already had 15 victories to his credit and who now shot down a reconnaissance Spitfire PR XIX (of No 683 Sqn) on 24 August, followed by a 339th FG P-51D Mustang (the first of its kind to succumb to an Me 262) on 11 September.

Leutnant Alfred Schreiber also claimed two further victories to add to his opening pair. Some doubt surrounds the first of these, which was reportedly a Spitfire intercepted on 26 August. But the destruction of the second – a Spitfire PR XI of the USAAF's 7th Photographic Reconnaissance Group (PRG), caught over Stuttgart on 5 September – was incontrovertible. Schreiber's gun camera showed that a burst of well-aimed 30 mm cannon fire, which could blow the wing off a B-17, could also shred a Spitfire to pieces (fortunately the American pilot managed to escape by parachute). The following day Oberfeldwebel Hubert Göbel (ex-JG 301) opened his jet scoreboard by downing yet another No 540 Sqn Mosquito PR XVI.

On 20 September 1944 Hitler conceded that the main emphasis of Me 262 production should be switched to fighters. Galland immediately began to redeploy his meagre forces. Exactly one week later the 'operational' components of EKdo 262 – the detachments at Rechlin-Lärz and Erfurt-Bindersleben, plus parts of those at Lechfeld – were ordered north to Achmer and Hesepe (neighbouring airfields near

This shot was one in a sequence of photographs taken of everyday scenes on the III./EJG 2 (III.*Ergänzungsjagdgeschwader* 2) ramp in late October 1944 at Lager-Lechfeld. This unit was formed with a large complement of Me 262A-1as on 27 October 1944, and it had the distinction of being the sole *Gruppe* of the five that comprised EJG 2 to equip with the turbojet-powered aircraft. Essentially a training unit, III./EJG 2's first *Kommandeur* was Hauptmann Horst Geyer, who remained with the *Gruppe* until 1 January 1945, when he was replaced by famous fighter *Experte*, Major Heinz Bär. The latter individual was credited with scoring 16 kills whilst flying the Me 262, most of which were achieved with III./EJG 2, prior to him joining JV 44 on 23 April 1945

Osnabrück), where they were to form the basis of a newer and larger fighter *Einsatzkommando*.

Meanwhile, the rump of EKdo 262's HQ staff, still commanded by Hauptmann Horst Geyer, would be incorporated into the newly established *Ergänzungsjagdgeschwader* (Operational Fighter Training Group) 2. This formation was made up of four component, but entirely separate, wings, each of which prepared trainee pilots for frontline service on a specific type of aircraft. Remaining at Lechfeld, Hauptmann Geyer's erstwhile EKdo 262 now became III./EJG 2, the official training establishment for all future Me 262 fighter pilots.

The importance of III./EJG 2's role was underlined on 4 November 1944 when the Führer, in a rare admission of his own fallibility, finally gave in to his experts' pleas. Henceforth (although by now far too late materially to affect the course of the war), the *entire* output of Me 262s would be fighters. In order to produce the pilots to fly them, it was planned for III./EJG 2 to have an establishment of 122 Me 262s, some four times the number of a standard operational *Gruppe*.

Reality fell far short of this. In the last week of November Hauptmann Geyer's Gruppe consisted of a dozen instructors, sixty-nine pupil pilots awaiting training . . . and just two Me 262s!

But by the month's end things were beginning to happen. Pupil ranks rose to 112 (with a corresponding increase in instructors to 26). More importantly, the number of Me 262s was increased to 23, including two of the very first dual-control two-seat trainers to be produced. On 1 December further organisational changes took place. Of III./EJG 2's three component *Staffeln*, 9./EJG 2 was equipped with a mix of piston-engined aircraft (for twin-engined familiarisation) and moved out to Landsberg. The other two *Staffeln* both operated the Me 262, 10./EJG 2 remaining at Lechfeld alongside the *Gruppenstab*, and 11./EJG 2 being redeployed at Unterschlauersbach, near Nuremberg.

The latter soon began to look upon themselves very much as second-

Another photograph in the Lager-Lechfeld sequence of late October 1944. III./EJG 2 flew its fleet of Me 262A-1as from dawn until dusk in a vain attempt to keep up with the demand by frontline units for barely-qualified jet pilots

Me 262A-2a bomber '9K+BK' of 2./KG 51 being towed from its camouflaged dispersal out onto the runway at Rheine in the late autumn of 1944. Note how the individual aircraft letter 'B' (red outlined in white) stands out, whereas the remainder of the code (in black, and about a quarter of the size) is to all intents and purposes invisible. Close scrutiny reveals that the nosecap, too, is painted red, which is again thinly ringed in white

class citizens. Compared to the acres of concrete at Lechfeld, Unterschlauersbach's grass runway quickly became inoperable in rain or snow; nose wheels dug in and accidents occurred with depressing regularity. 11. *Staffel* did not receive a single one of the *Gruppe*'s handful of Me 262B two-seat trainers (all of which were retained at Lechfeld), and they firmly believed that their complement of single-seaters was made entirely of Lechfeld's oldest and most worn out Messerschmitt jet fighters.

On paper, III./EJG 2's course of instruction on the Me 262 called for an initial 20 hours on piston-engined fighters. This was intended primarily for the conversion of ex-bomber pilots, for which purpose the *Gruppe* was equipped with about a dozen late variant Bf 109Gs and Ks, plus four or five Fw 190S two-seat trainers. During this stage the pupils also received three days' theoretical tuition on the Me 262's cockpit layout, flight characteristics and the all-important smooth throttle control required by the jet engines. Unlike a propeller-driven fighter, the throttle could not simply be rammed to the firewall, but had to be treated with much more circumspection and finesse – 'A piston-engined fighter will tolerate a slow thinking pilot with quick reactions; the Me 262 demands the exact opposite'.

On take-off, for example, power input had to be gradual until sufficient speed had been built up to be able to climb away. Likewise when landing, the necessarily slow and controlled reduction of power (to prevent flame-out) committed the Me 262 to a lengthy approach. It was this vulnerability at low-level which was pounced upon by Allied fighter pilots as the Achilles' heel of the jet, and which would lead to the Luftwaffe mounting standing patrols by piston-engined fighters over the Me 262 bases to protect the jets as they took off and landed.

Such dangers were still some weeks away, however, as III./EJG 2's pupils were next posted to Landsberg. Here, they underwent some ten hours of twin-engined training on 9. *Staffel*'s mix of Focke-Wulf Fw 58s, Siebel Si 204s and Messerschmitt Bf 110s. A lucky few even made the acquaintance of a tricycle undercarriage when scheduled to fly the unit's sole Ta 154, an unsuccessful Focke-Wulf nightfighter design.

Only after this did the trainees return to Lechfeld, or depart for Unterschlauersbach, and actually get their hands on an Me 262. An introductory period devoted to ground taxying was followed by two half-hour sessions of circuits and bumps. Then came an hour each of general handling and manoeuvring, of high-altitude flight (up to 8000 metres) and cross-country navigation. A further two hours of formation flying, at first led by an instructor but latterly in all-pupil *Rotten* or *Ketten* (formations of two or three aircraft), prepared trainees for the final stage of the course. This was gunnery practice, both air-to-air (against towed drogues) and air-to-ground over the nearby ranges.

Needless to say, the well-ordered training régime outlined above did not survive intact for long in the increasingly chaotic conditions of that last winter of the war. A combination of bad weather, prowling Allied fighter-bombers and, ultimately, an acute shortage of aviation fuel (supplies to training units were reduced drastically following an OKL directive of 13 February 1945), soon led to disruptions. Nevertheless, III./EJG 2 continued to turn out a steady flow of 'qualified' jet pilots.

There were, of course, the inevitable casualties, as was to be expected of any training programme. But remarkably few of the trainees actually fell victim to enemy fighters. Perhaps even more surprisingly, a number of claims were made by the *Gruppe*. One of the first recorded instances was the Fifteenth AF P-38 Lightning shot down by Leutnant Rudolf Harbort on 5 February 1945. The following month Hauptmann Wilhelm Steinmann's four victories (two P-51s and two B-17s) fell just short of making him a jet ace, but were a fitting climax to a Luftwaffe career which had begun in 1936, and which included 40 piston-engined kills while serving with JGs 27 and 4.

It was in March, too, that an even better-known ex-Fw 190 'Experte', Oberst Walther Dahl (see *Aircraft of the Aces 9 - Fw 190 Aces of the Western Front*), added two Me 262 kills to his score of 126 by downing a brace of P-47s in a single day during his belated transition.

But III./EJG 2 did produce one undisputed ace who alone was responsible for claiming nearly one third of the *Gruppe*'s estimated 40 victories. Heinz Bär's first kill had been achieved on 25 September 1939 while serving as an Unteroffizier on the western front with JG 51. Since that date his number of victories had climbed steadily, although his rise through the ranks had not always progressed with equal smoothness (see *Aircraft of the Aces 9 - Fw 190 Aces of the Western Front* and *11- Bf 109D/E Aces 1939-41*).

On 1 January 1945 Major Heinz Bär, now with a tally of 204 kills, had taken over command of III./EJG 2 from Hauptmann Geyer. This appointment, from *Geschwaderkommodore* of JG 3 to the lower post of a *Gruppenkommandeur*, might have been construed as yet another demotion in the outspoken Bär's see-saw career. In fact, it was an inspired choice. The thankless, but vital, task of continuing to train

Despite their being a purely bomber unit, some pilots of KG 51 did try – or were forced – to 'mix it'. Here, early in October 1944, Leutnant Joachim Fingerlos of 3.*Staffel* in '9K+XL' chases a USAAF P-51D (just visible in the top right-hand corner of the photo) near Rheine, unaware of another Mustang closing in on his own tail. Seconds later Fingerlos' starboard engine was hit and exploded in a mass of flames. He bailed out seriously wounded, having fallen victim to Lt C W Mueller of the 353rd FG

21

pilots for the Luftwaffe's élite jet fighter units whilst all around was collapsing in ruins, required a man of 'Pritzl' Bär's calibre.

Although always one to lead by example, the administrative demands of Bär's new position kept him firmly anchored to the ground for the first few weeks. It was not until 29 January that he made his premier flight as *Kommandeur* of III./EJG 2. Thereafter, 'Buzzard 1' – Bär's tactical call sign – was in the air almost daily; undertaking some 80-90 sorties in all while with the *Gruppe*. His first recorded jet victory (a P-51D) was claimed following an emergency scramble from Lechfeld shortly after midday on 19 March 1945 – his 436th mission of the war. Forty-eight hours later he brought down a B-24D. Another Liberator and a P-51D, claimed on 24 March, preceded a remarkable succession of doubles in April – two B-26s on the 9th, two P-47s on the 18th and two P-51Ds on the 19th.

Heinz Bär had full confidence in the Me 262's superiority;

'The jet was just too much for an enemy single-engined fighter to handle. On the other hand, we could choose to accept or refuse combat. It was entirely up to us. The edge in performance and hitting power given to us by the Me 262 was decisive.'

But Bär was aware of the jet's shortcomings too;

'We were in real trouble if we lost an engine. And it was a petrifying experience to be low on fuel, preparing to land, and suddenly discover that Allied fighters had followed you home!'

It was not Allied fighters which wrote *finis* to III./EJG 2's brief six months' existence, however, but the approach of ground troops of General Patch's Seventh US Army. Lechfeld was evacuated on 23 April, the *Gruppe* withdrawing to Munich-Riem from where (training being no longer possible) those pupils considered sufficiently proficient on the Me 262, plus a number of instructors, were posted on northeastwards to Prague-Ruzyn and JG 7. A smaller number, including Oberstleutnant Heinz Bär, remained at Munich-Riem to swell the ranks of Generalleutnant Adolf Galland's JV 44.

Meanwhile, what of those 'operational' components of the original EKdo 262 which, back in September 1944, had not been earmarked for incorporation into III./EJG 2 at Lechfeld, but had instead been deployed northwards to Achmer and Hesepe to form a new *Einsatzkommando*?

This latter was to be Galland's showpiece unit, offering proof positive that the Me 262 could – and should – play a dominant role in the fighter defence of the Reich. But the *Einsatzkommando* had three strikes against it from the start. Firstly, its 30 assigned aircraft (more accurately, perhaps, their Junkers Jumo powerplants) were by no stretch of the imagination operationally ready, or reli-

The weapon – a close-up of the compact low-velocity MK 108 cannon with one of its 30 mm high-explosive shells. Four of these guns were grouped in the nose of the Me 262, each firing at a rate of 660 rounds per minute . . .

. . . and the damage it inflicted. Although of poor quality, this photograph graphically illustrates just how effective the weapon was against the B-17. Note the destroyed tailgun position, the shredded starboard tailplane and damage to both wings. This 305th BG Flying Fortress is, in fact, the one attacked by the Me 163 flown by Leutnant Hartmut Ryll on 16 August 1944 – see page 83, top, and colour profile number 30

able. Secondly, only some 50 per cent of its pilots – those previously members of EKdo 262 – had sufficient jet experience. The remainder had been hurriedly drafted in after only two, or at most three, perfunctory familiarisation flights on the Me 262 at Lechfeld or Rechlin.

These two disadvantages may have been unavoidable under the current circumstances. The third – the choice of the twin airfields at Achmer and Hesepe as the *Kommando*'s operating bases – was a major blunder. Although both possessed the long concrete runways essential for jet operations, their location, some 5 km apart, and approximately 15 km north-northwest of Osnabrück, placed them directly under the flightpath of one of the main approach routes used by USAAF heavy bombers attacking central Germany and Berlin . . . and a route, moreover, which the Eighth AF's fighters were now in the habit of scouring, ahead of the bomber stream, to suppress any likely opposition.

To counter these perceived handicaps Galland selected one of his most able and successful combat leaders to head the new *Kommando*. Austrian-born Major Walter Nowotny was one of the foremost *Experten* of the Russian front. He had been the first pilot in the Luftwaffe to achieve 250 kills (on 14 October 1943, for which he had been awarded the Diamonds to the Oak Leaves and Swords of his Knight's Cross – see *Aircraft of the Aces 6 - Fw 190 Aces of the Russian Front*). In February 1944 he was withdrawn from frontline service by special Order of the Führer and appointed Kommodore of JG 101, a fighter training *Geschwader* based at Pau. This quiet backwater at the foot of the French Pyrenees was not at all to Nowotny's liking, but while there he had been summoned briefly to Lechfeld to test-fly the Me 262. And on 20 September he gladly relinquished command of JG 101 to take over the newly-established, two-*Staffel* strong, jet unit, which inevitably became known as the *Kommando Nowotny*.

As eager as Galland himself to make a success of the Luftwaffe's first 'operational' jet fighter commando, Nowotny wasted no time. Upon being introduced to Oberleutnant Hans-Günter Müller, CO of the Hesepe *Staffel*, Nowotny's reaction was immediate;

'What? You are the *Staffelkapitän* and you still haven't scored a single kill on the Me 262? I suggest you find yourself some other employment in the defence of the Reich organisation!'

Having already made clear his intention of gathering as many as possible of his old JG 54 eastern front comrades around him, Nowotny immediately sent for one such to replace the hapless Müller. Knight's Cross holder Oberleutnant Alfred Teumer was a long-serving member of JG 54 with 76 victories to his credit. After the briefest of conversions on to the Me 262 at Rechlin, Teumer flew in to Hesepe on 4 October. But on final approach his machine suffered an engine failure. The inexperienced pilot's attempt at a single-engined landing was unsuccessful and he was killed in the resulting crash. This was but the first of a series of losses (both accidental and in combat) which, in little more than a month, would see the brave, but ill-starred experiment that was the *Kommando Nowotny*, reduced from 30 aircraft to just 4!

Although far from operational, the *Kommando*'s first combat sorties were flown on 7 October against bombers returning from raids on oil targets within the Reich. At Hesepe, Teumer's successor, Leutnant Franz Schall (another Soviet front Knight's Cross *Experte*, although this time ex-JG 52), scrambled with EKdo 262 'veteran' Feldwebel Helmut Lennartz as his wingman. Each claimed a B-24D destroyed.

But it was a different story at Achmer. There, *Staffelkapitän* Oberleutnant Paul Bley was just taking off, with Leutnant Gerhard Kobert and Oberfähnrich Heinz Russel in attendance, when all three were jumped by enemy fighters. Bley and Kobert both fell victim to

The first in a sequence of shots of III./EJG 2's 'White 10' (Wk-Nr. 110 926 – not to be confused with the aircraft pictured on page 16, despite the superficially similar markings), as flown by Leutnant Kurt Bell during the making of a Luftwaffe training film. First, Bell is cleared for take-off by a flag-waving Luftwaffe female auxiliary, whose hair style, one suspects, would cause any self-respecting WAAF flight sergeant to have an apoplectic fit!

the same P-51D, flown by 20-year-old Lt Urban Drew of the 361st FG (see Osprey's *Me 262 - Stormbird Rising* for more details) – this double success took Drew's tally to six kills, thus making him an ace.

Caught at their most vulnerable (at low level, nursing their throttles, and unable either to jink violently or climb steeply away), the *Jagdflieger* were sitting ducks. And although Bley managed to bale out of his stricken, inverted aircraft and lived to fight another day (another three weeks, to be exact), Kobert stood no chance when his machine was hit in the main fuel tank and exploded in a huge ball of orange flame. The third of the trio, Oberfähnrich Russel, had not yet lifted off when his undercarriage was shot out from under him. His Me 262 slid along the runway in a shower of sparks before coming to a halt. Russel, too, succeeded in escaping before the wreckage went up in flames.

As a direct result of these losses, two *Staffeln* of Fw 190D-9s were assigned to the *Kommando* to fly standing patrols during the jets' take-off and landing runs – 9. and 10./JG 54 took up residence at Achmer and Hesepe respectively. On 12 October 9.*Staffel* lost six of its Fw 190s whilst flying cover for Me 262s scrambling from Achmer. In return, Bley and Lennartz each claimed a P-51D apiece, but then they too both damaged their aircraft in forced landings away from the base.

The Fw 190s may have been able to offer some protection against prowling Allied fighters (albeit at a price!), but they were powerless to

Once aloft, 'White 10' displays all the aura of deadly elegance which typified the Me 262 when in its natural element . . .

. . . before the wheels come down to begin the long, gradual descent to the runway threshold. It was at this point that the Me 262 was at its most vulnerable

25

stop the accidents which whittled away at the *Kommando*'s strength. On 13 October two more Me 262s were written off. It was after this that Nowotny imposed a two-week ban on operational flying while Messerschmitt representatives sought to evaluate the technical and tactical experience gained to date. They found it a sobering exercise.

When operations resumed on 28 October the *Kommando*'s fortunes were as mixed as ever. On that date Leutnant Schreiber downed a P-38 and Leutnant Schall a P-51D. Against that, Schall's own machine was damaged landing back at Hesepe with a jammed nose wheel. And at Achmer *Staffelkapitän* Oberleutnant Bley had discovered to his cost that lurking Allied fighters were not the only danger laying in wait for the unwary. On take-off he had collided with a pile-driver working on the foundations of a new building being constructed just beyond the airfield's perimeter. After having been involved in four crashes in five take-offs, this was finally the one Bley did not walk away from. His place was immediately filled by Oberleutnant Georg-Peter Eder, *Kapitän*-in-waiting of the *Kommando*'s planned third *Staffel* which, in the event, was never to be formed.

And so it went on. On 29 October two NCO pilots claimed a P-47 each, while the seemingly indefatigable Schreiber first destroyed a reconnaissance Lightning (designated F-5) and then had to take to his own parachute after colliding with a Spitfire. Another five USAAF fighters were downed in the week that followed, but at a cost of ten of the *Kommando*'s rapidly dwindling stock of Me 262s. Oberfähnrich Willi Banzhaff was shot down twice – he baled out after clashing with Eighth AF fighters over Holland on 1 November, only to succumb to an RAF Tempest over Lüneburg heath 48 hours later. Three more jets were written off in forced or single-engined landings, and another five were damaged to a lesser degree.

At the controls of Me 262 V 167 Wk-Nr 130167 is test pilot Gerd Lindner. This aircraft was employed specifically for stability investigations. Seen taxying back to its dispersal following the completion of yet another test flight, V 167 was cpatured on film in December 1944 whilst participating in fighter-bomber trials

On 7 November Adolf Galland visited the *Kommando*. He had invited Generaloberst Alfred Keller to accompany him. 'Bomben' Keller (literally 'bomb cellar', i.e. air raid shelter), as he was universally known throughout the Luftwaffe, was head of the NSFK (National Socialist Flying Corps). It was the latter's presence which prompted Major Nowotny to order an all-out effort the following morning when USAAF bombers were reported to be approaching. It was indicative of the low level to which the unit had sunk that this 'effort' turned out to be just four machines – two each from Achmer and Hesepe.

But even this proved overly optimistic. At Achmer Walter Nowotny, whose first combat mission on the Me 262 this was to be, could not get his engines to start, while Feldwebel Erich Büttner, one of the Hesepe *Rotte*, burst a tyre during taxying which resulted in the undercarriage leg being pushed up through his wing. Thus only Oberleutnant Günther Wegmann, Nowotny's wingman, and the Hesepe leader, Leutnant Schall, actually managed to get airborne and engage the enemy, bringing down a P-47 and a P-51D respectively.

By the time the bombers were on their return flight, however, the fault in Nowotny's machine had been rectified. In the early afternoon he finally took off, followed by Leutnant Franz Schall, and disappeared into the almost unbroken layer of low cloud to engage the unseen bomber stream flying some 30,000 ft above. Schall never

The experimental Me 262C-1a *'Heimatschützer I'* ('Homeland Protector I'), which had a Walter 509A-2 rocket motor installed in the rear fuselage. It was in this aircraft (Wk-Nr 130186 – see profile number 7) that Oberstleutnant Heinz Bär, *Gruppenkommandeur* of III./EJG 2, reputedly shot down a P-47 Thunderbolt in early March 1945, shortly before the jet was itself destroyed on the ground during a low-level Allied fighter sweep. The rocket exhaust (and the need for the cutaway rudder!) is clearly visible as V 186 begins its take-off run

Major Walter Nowotny, the 258-victory Russian front ace, and holder of the Knight's Cross with Oak Leaves, Swords and Diamonds, was killed on his first operational jet sortie on 8 November 1944

got through to the bombers, but claimed two P-51Ds destroyed before suffering engine failure at high altitude. Pointing his nose earthwards, Schall tried desperately to restart his engines, but before he could do so he was pounced upon by other Mustangs and forced to bale out.

The exact circumstances surrounding the end of Walter Nowotny remain uncertain to this day. Those on the ground clearly heard the sound of combat above the clouds – the chatter of machine-gun fire, the duller thumps of an Me 262's cannon – and Nowotny radioed that he had downed a B-24D (probably a B-17G) and probably destroyed a P-51D. But then he reported the failure of one engine before making one final garbled transmission which contained the word 'burning'.

Whether Nowotny's loss was caused by yet another of the catastrophic engine failures which had plagued his *Kommando* throughout its short history, or whether his death was attributable to enemy fighters (only in recent years have US historians proposed that Nowotny's victor was P-51D pilot Lt Robert W Stevens of the 364th FG, and even this suggestion has been provisionally, rather than categorically, stated in light of the available evidence) or 'friendly' flak is a moot point. The result, however, is not in question. Many witnesses observed the Me 262 dive vertically out of the clouds and smash into the ground at Epe, some 2.5 kilometres east of Hesepe. Among the onlookers was Adolf Galland, who promptly appointed Oberleutnant Georg-Peter Eder to replace Nowotny.

But the *Kommando* did not long survive its eponymous leader. The now Hauptmann Eder flew a few more sorties from Achmer, including that on 13 November during which he scored his first jet kill 'almost by accident', as he later reported;

'I had been sent up against a high-flying reconnaissance Lightning. Ground control did a wonderful job, although it wasn't hard for me to spot him as he was pulling a thick contrail. I approached him from slightly above and out of the sun. At about 800 metres I eased down

Kommando Nowotny line-up, reportedly photographed at Achmer in late September 1944. 'White 19' and 'White 4' are being serviced in the background as a Kettenkrad (motorcycle half-track) tows 'Green 3' out onto the runway

Close-up detail of 'White 4'. The typical *Kommando Nowotny* finish of fairly solid fuselage colour, worn in conjunction with distinctively dappled vertical tail surfaces, is clearly apparent

Leutnant Franz Schall's pilotless Me 262 (note missing cockpit canopy!) was photographed by P-51D pilot Lt James W Kenney of the 357th FG during the disastrous 8 November 1944 sortie in which Walter Nowotny was killed (see opposite). Although Kenney was officially credited with the destruction of Schall's aircraft, two other American pilots also chased the machine as it glided earthwards, claiming a half-kill apiece when they saw it suddenly roll onto its back and spin into the ground

The photos on this page show KG 51 Me 262A-1a Wk-Nr 110813 being bombed up by armourers during the early months of 1945. This jet first flew at Leipheim in December 1944, being initially issued to III./EJG 2 prior to its transfer to KG 51 'Edelweiss'

into the contrail immediately behind him. A quick check of my guns and the engine instruments. But I must have misjudged my closing speed, for when I looked up again a second later the Lightning was filling my windscreen – bigger than any aircraft I had ever had in front of me. I tried to pull up over him, but it was too late. There was an almighty crash, and he disappeared. I waited a few seconds for something to happen – a wing to fall off or an engine to quit – but, apart from a few large dents, all was well and the crate continued to fly.'

Not so the P-38, which reportedly crashed near Schleissheim.

On 17 November, by which time the majority of the pilots had been withdrawn to Lechfeld for re-equipment, Eder flew the *Kommando*'s last mission out of Achmer. Forty-eight hours later he, and they, were to form the nucleus of the III. *Gruppe* of the Luftwaffe's one, and only, true jet fighter *Geschwader* – JG 7.

COLOUR PLATES

This 11-page colour section profiles many of the aircraft flown by the leading Luftwaffe jet aces of 1944-45, as well as the mounts of some of the lesser known pilots who scored five or more kills. All the artwork has been specially commissioned for this volume, and profile artist (and co-author) John Weal and figure artist Mike Chappell have gone to great pains to illustrate the aircraft, and their pilots, as accurately as possible following exhaustive research. Almost all of the Me 262s, Me 163s, He 162s and the sole Ar 234 depicted on the following pages have never been illustrated in colour before, and the schemes shown have been fully authenticated either by surviving *jagdflieger* from the period, or contemporary photographs taken by Luftwaffe personnel or Allied troops.

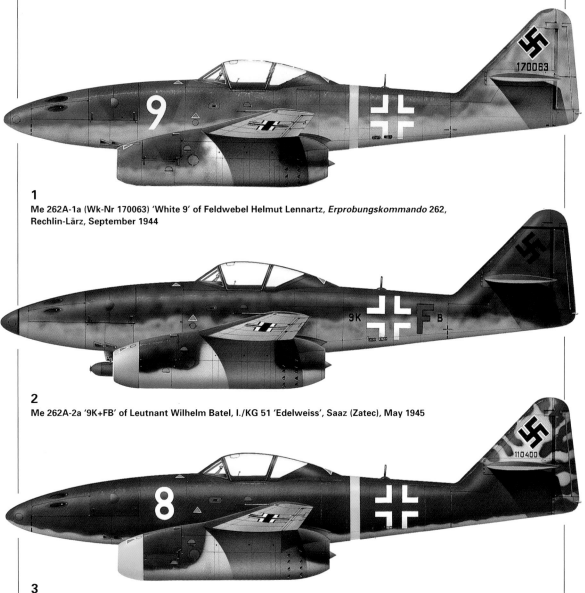

1
Me 262A-1a (Wk-Nr 170063) 'White 9' of Feldwebel Helmut Lennartz, *Erprobungskommando* 262, Rechlin-Lärz, September 1944

2
Me 262A-2a '9K+FB' of Leutnant Wilhelm Batel, I./KG 51 'Edelweiss', Saaz (Zatec), May 1945

3
Me 262A-1a (Wk-Nr 110400) 'White 8' of Major Walter Nowotny, *KdoFührer* of the *Kommando Nowotny*, Achmer, November 1944

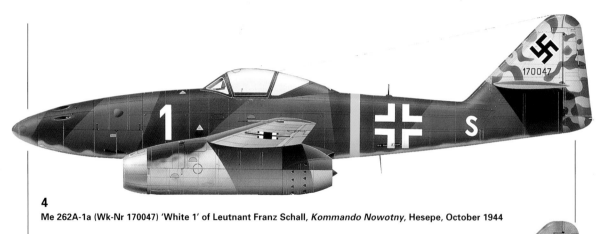

4
Me 262A-1a (Wk-Nr 170047) 'White 1' of Leutnant Franz Schall, *Kommando Nowotny*, Hesepe, October 1944

5
Me 262A-1a (Wk-Nr 110372) 'White 3' of Leutnant Alfred Schreiber, *Kommando Nowotny*, Achmer, November 1944

6
Me 262A-1a (Wk-Nr 110559) 'Red 13' of Oberstleutnant Heinz Bär, *Kommandeur* III./EJG 2, Lechfeld, March 1945

7

Me 262C-1a (Wk-Nr 130186) 'V186' flown by Oberstleutnant Heinz Bär, *Kommandeur* III./EJG 2, Lechfeld, March 1945

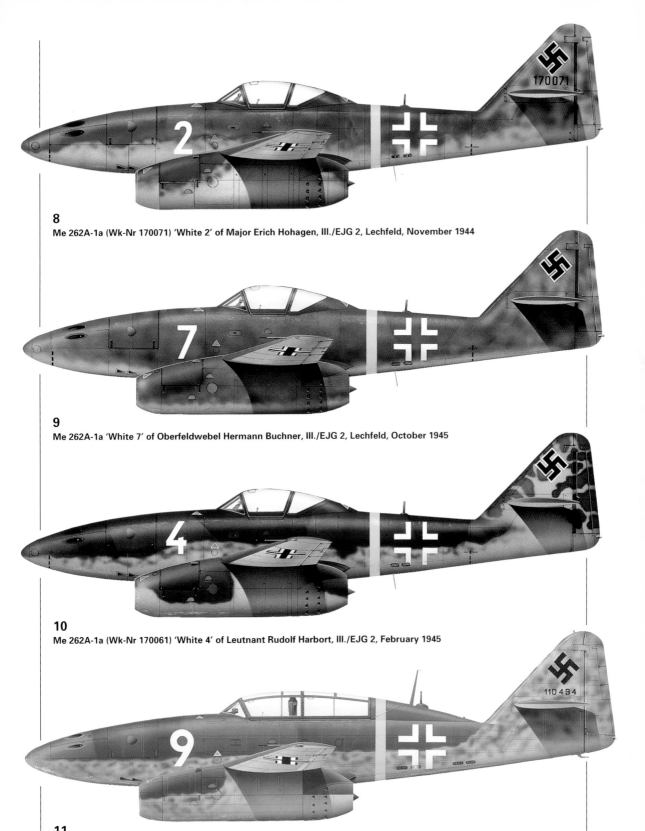

8
Me 262A-1a (Wk-Nr 170071) 'White 2' of Major Erich Hohagen, III./EJG 2, Lechfeld, November 1944

9
Me 262A-1a 'White 7' of Oberfeldwebel Hermann Buchner, III./EJG 2, Lechfeld, October 1945

10
Me 262A-1a (Wk-Nr 170061) 'White 4' of Leutnant Rudolf Harbort, III./EJG 2, February 1945

11
Me 262B-1a (Wk-Nr 110494) 'White 9' of Gefreiter Ferdinand Sagemeister, III./EJG 2, Lechfeld, December 1944

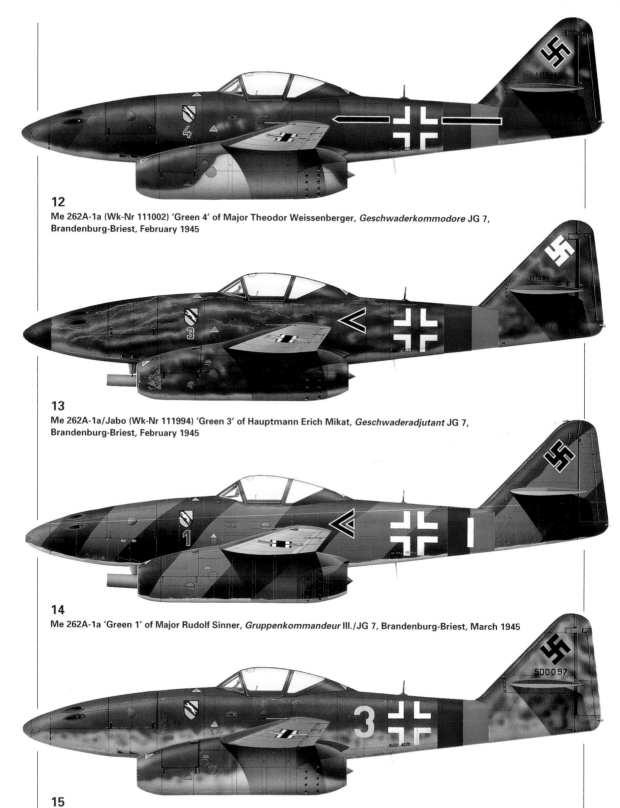

12
Me 262A-1a (Wk-Nr 111002) 'Green 4' of Major Theodor Weissenberger, *Geschwaderkommodore* JG 7, Brandenburg-Briest, February 1945

13
Me 262A-1a/Jabo (Wk-Nr 111994) 'Green 3' of Hauptmann Erich Mikat, *Geschwaderadjutant* JG 7, Brandenburg-Briest, February 1945

14
Me 262A-1a 'Green 1' of Major Rudolf Sinner, *Gruppenkommandeur* III./JG 7, Brandenburg-Briest, March 1945

15
Me 262A-1a (Wk.-Nr. 500097) 'Yellow 3' of Oberleutnant Hans Waldmann, *Staffelkapitän* 3./JG 7, Kaltenkirchen, March 1945

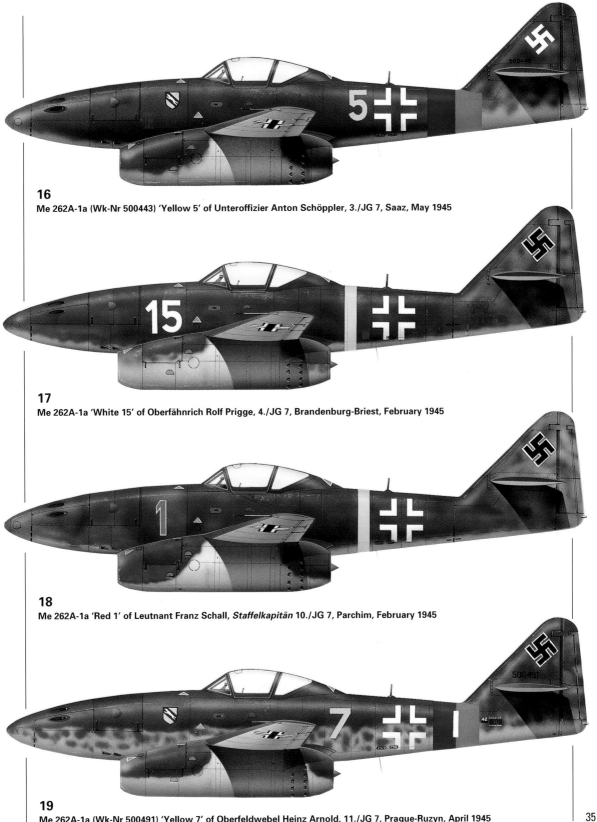

16
Me 262A-1a (Wk-Nr 500443) 'Yellow 5' of Unteroffizier Anton Schöppler, 3./JG 7, Saaz, May 1945

17
Me 262A-1a 'White 15' of Oberfähnrich Rolf Prigge, 4./JG 7, Brandenburg-Briest, February 1945

18
Me 262A-1a 'Red 1' of Leutnant Franz Schall, *Staffelkapitän* 10./JG 7, Parchim, February 1945

19
Me 262A-1a (Wk-Nr 500491) 'Yellow 7' of Oberfeldwebel Heinz Arnold, 11./JG 7, Prague-Ruzyn, April 1945

20
Me 262A-1a (Wk-Nr 501221) 'Yellow 3' of Oberfeldwebel Hermann Buchner, III./JG 7, Prague-Ruzyn, April 1945

21
Me 262B-1a/U1 (Wk-Nr 111980) 'Red 12' of Leutnant Herbert Altner, 10./NJG 11, Reinfeld (nr. Lübeck), May 1945

22
Me 262A-1a 'White 3' of Generalleutnant Adolf Galland, *Verbandsführer* JV 44, Munich-Riem, April 1945

23
Me 262A-1a/U4 (Wk-Nr 111899) of Major Wilhelm Herget, JV 44, Munich-Riem, April 1945

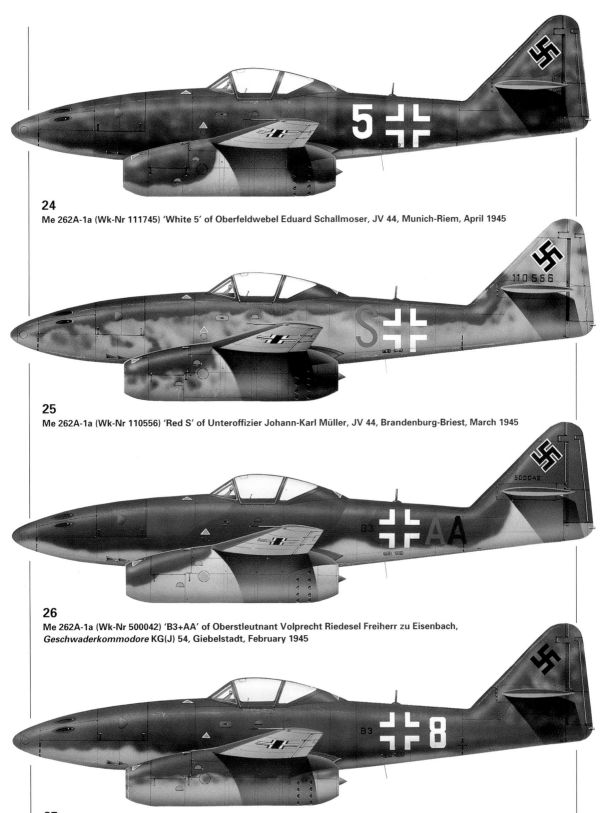

24
Me 262A-1a (Wk-Nr 111745) 'White 5' of Oberfeldwebel Eduard Schallmoser, JV 44, Munich-Riem, April 1945

25
Me 262A-1a (Wk-Nr 110556) 'Red S' of Unteroffizier Johann-Karl Müller, JV 44, Brandenburg-Briest, March 1945

26
Me 262A-1a (Wk-Nr 500042) 'B3+AA' of Oberstleutnant Volprecht Riedesel Freiherr zu Eisenbach,
Geschwaderkommodore KG(J) 54, Giebelstadt, February 1945

27
Me 262A-1a 'B3+white 8' of Hauptmann Werner Tronicke, *Staffelkapitän* 1./KG(J) 54, Zerbst, April 1945

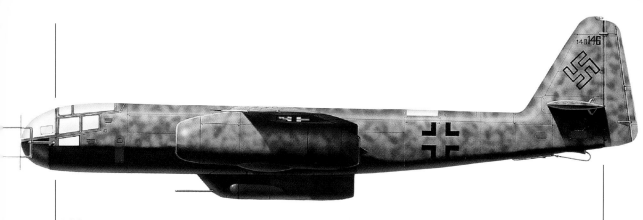

28
Ar 234B-2 (Wk-Nr 140146) of Hauptmann Kurt Bonow, *KdoFührer* of the *Kommando Bonow*, Oranienburg, March 1945

29
Me 163B-0 V41 'PK+QL' of Major Wolfgang Späte, *KdoFührer* of *Erprobungskommando* 16, Bad Zwischenahn, May 1944

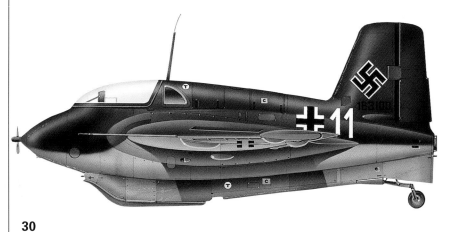

30
Me 163B (Wk-Nr 163100) 'White 11' of Leutnant Hartmut Ryll, 1./JG 400, Brandis, August 1944

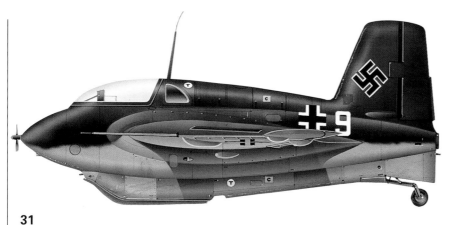

31
Me 163B 'White 9' of Leutnant Fritz Kelb, 1./JG 400, Brandis, January 1945

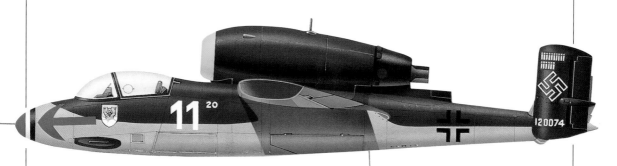

32
He 162A-2 (Wk-Nr 120074) 'White 11' of Oberleutnant Emil Demuth, *Staffelkapitän* 3./JG 1, Leck, May 1945

33
He 162A-2 (Wk-Nr 120027?) 'White 1' of Leutnant Rudolf Schmitt, 1./JG 1, Leck, May 1945

1
Major Georg-Peter Eder,
Staffelkapitän 9./JG 7, Parchim,
February 1945

2
Generalleutnant Adolf Galland,
Kommandeur JV 44, Munich-Riem,
April 1945

3
Leutnant Karl 'Quax' Schnörrer, JG 7,
Munich-Riem, March 1945

4
Oberleutnant Kurt Welter,
Staffelkapitän 10./NJG 11
(*Kommando Welter*), Burg, near
Magdeburg, April 1945

5
Major Wolfgang Späte,
Geschwaderkommodore JG 400,
Brandis, April 1945

6
Hauptmann Franz Schall,
Staffelkapitän 10./JG 7, Parchim,
March 1945

JG 7 – THE MAIN PROTAGONIST

J G 7 holds the distinction of being the most prolific operator of the Me 262. Let us consider the specific features pertaining to this *Jagdgeschwader* which confirm its position as the premier user of Messerschmitt's revolutionary jet fighter. JG 7 was the first frontline fighter unit to equip with the aircraft, and during the seven months of its existence, it received more Me 262s, and pilots, than any other *Geschwader*. As a result of its relative strength in numbers, JG 7 was also responsible for producing the bulk of the Luftwaffe's jet aces.

As noted earlier in this volume, the effectiveness of the Me 262 as a potentially war-winning design had been recognised as early as the spring of 1943 when leading Luftwaffe fighter pilots Hauptmann Wolfgang Späte and Generalleutnant Adolf Galland were given the opportunity to test-fly a prototype aircraft. Späte first flew an Me 262 on 17 April, whilst Galland evaluated the Me 262 V4 five weeks later. The jet fighter was to leave a lasting impression on Galland, who not only saw its potential, but towards the end of the war would himself become a jet ace (as did Späte) at the controls of a production Me 262.

FALSE START

JG 7 was formed in August 1944 with the express purpose of operating two *Gruppen* of Fw 190s from Königsberg. A paucity of pilots and aircraft put paid to these plans, however, and it was decided instead to

This Me 262A-1a was reportedly flown by Major Theodor Weissenberger, *Kommandeur* of I./JG 7 at Lechfeld late in 1944. Unfortunately, the unit badge is indecipherable on the original print, and although the presentation of the small numeral below the shield is indicative of JG 7's *Stab* machines (see profile numbers 12 to 14), other sources suggest this may be an aircraft of KG 51

11./JG 7 pilots pose for a group photo taken at Brandenburg-Briest in February 1945. From left to right are Oberfeldwebel Heinz Arnold (KIA), Unteroffizier Heine Geisthövel (KIA), Feldwebel Franz Köster, Unteroffizier Hellmut Detjens, Leutnant Joachim Weber (KIA), Unteroffizier Ernst Giefing, Feldwebel Wilhelm Bergmann, Feldwebel Heinz Eichner (KIA), Oberfeldwebel A Lübking (KIA) and Leutnant Fritz R G Müller (*via Hellmut Detjens*)

equip the two *Gruppen* with Bf 109G-14s and operate II. *Gruppe* from the Czechoslovakian airfield of Ziegenhain. Just as the planned Fw 190 re-equipment had fallen foul of the acute shortage of pilots and aircraft, so too the revised OKL orders for issuing the new *Jagdgeschwader* with the Bf 109G-14 was also scrapped.

Despite these setbacks, Oberst Johannes 'Macki' Steinhoff was brought in to command JG 7, and events seemed to immediately take a dramatic turn for the better as the *Geschwader* was expanded to include three *Gruppen*, all of which were to be equipped with the new turbojet-powered Messerschmitt Me 262. Postwar, Steinhoff recalled the first days of the establishment of the world's premier jet *Geschwader* during the late autumn of 1944;

'The first machines began to arrive. They came in sections on long railway trucks from the south of the Reich, and the mechanics, assisted by a team from the Messerschmitt works, started assembling them and shooting in the cannon. By the end of November we were in the air, training in flights of three and in small formations.'

After six weeks of flying training at Brandenburg-Briest, Steinhoff finally began to feel that JG 7 was close to reaching operational status. New aircraft, problems with the supply of specialised parts and the arrival of new pilots meant that it took time for Steinhoff to mould JG 7 into anything like a cohesive unit. Indeed, this lack of operational togetherness was to blight the *Geschwader* for the rest of the war. Typically, JG 7's pilots fought under conditions of extreme stress and frenetic activity, with inadequately trained pilots often being thrust into action before they had even mastered flying the jet, let alone how to fight and survive in it when engaging the enemy.

By the second week of November, JG 7's core of officer and NCO pilots had gathered at the 'Silber' ('Silver') airfield of Lager-Lechfeld, in

Wearing a woollen skull cap to protect his recently-healed head wound, Major Erich Hohagen is seen undergoing jet training at Lager-Lechfeld in late 1944. His conversion training was scant to say the least, but he was neverthelss so impressed by the new jet that he is quoted as having said that the advent of the Me 262 was 'the biggest step since the Wright brothers flew an aircraft heavier than air'

the heart of Bavaria. Many of these men had already enjoyed years of success on piston-engined fighters, and one of them, Hermann Buchner, recorded that as many as 70 per cent of the pilots were aces. With such a body of experienced *Jagdflieger*, it became quickly apparent that the pilots anticipated taking their new machines into action at the earliest opportunity. It was not to be, however, for at the first sign of an air raid, the Me 262s were usually pushed under the nearest tree in the hollow of the airstrip of Lager-Lechfeld, and the pilots ordered to exit to the nearest slit trenches. Morale was not helped by such orders, and the pilots, under the leadership of Rudi Sinner, gained the concession from their superiors that a *Schwarm* would be kept 'at readiness' in order to scramble should enemy aircraft be detected.

The *Schwarm* first saw action on 28 November, four pilots, including Sinner and Buchner, being involved – Major Sinner was the *Schwarmführer* (leader of the four aircraft) and Oberfeldwebel Buchner his *Rottenführer* (leader of the pair). The following account of this historic sortie is based on information gleaned by the authors from Buchner himself.

The weather was not too brilliant when take-off was ordered at approximately 1115. The small Riedel starter motor fitted in Buchner's Me 262 began to chatter, and the pilot was fortunate that his engines caught first time and ran smoothly, unlike the remaining three *Jagdflieger* within the alert *Schwarm*, all of whom experienced problems which effectively meant that none of their Jumo 004 turbojets started. A decision was quickly reached that Buchner would have to go it alone.

As his undercarriage retracted after successfully negotiating the take-off, Buchner checked his instruments – especially the engine temperature gauges – and tuned his FuG 14 radio to channel 'Bavaria' (the frequency on which his ground controllers operated). He then made the brief communication, 'Swallow to "Bavaria". Come in please'. After a momentary delay 'Bavaria' replied with their first instructions. By this time, Buchner (in Me 262A-1a 'Yellow 8') had reached an altitude of some 5000 to 6000 metres, and he was swiftly vectored towards a USAAF reconnaissance aircraft being tracked in the Munich sector – this sortie was not only the pilot's first on type, but also his first under the direction of a ground-control *Jägerleitoffizier*!

'Fly Caruso 340. Hanni 7000. Bird ahead 200' ('Course 340°. Height 7000 metres. Target 20 km ahead'). By now Buchner was at the correct height and on course, with his distance to the target rapidly diminishing. The pilot released the safety catches for the fighter's quartet of 30 mm Rheinmetall Borsig MK 108 cannon and checked the engine gauges one more time.

Buchner then received another message from 'Bavaria'. 'Bird ahead Five, four, three, two, one. You have contact!' His eyes swept the skies to check that no other enemy aircraft were in the vicinity. This first contact came to nothing, however, and as the pilot could not locate the enemy aircraft, he awaited further instructions. By this time Buchner had been in the Munich area for about 15 minutes. When the second communication from ground-control came through, he found this to be equally unrewarding in respect to achieving an interception. Buchner was puzzled, for he was an experienced operational pilot and felt confident in command of the Me 262.

Having checked his instruments once again, yet another new vector crackled through his headset direct from the Munich ground-controllers. 'Fly Caruso 270'. After a few minutes, ground-control came on again 'Am passing you over to "Leander"' ('Leander' being Stuttgart ground-control).

Over Augsburg a sheet of stratus was piling in from west to east. Soon Buchner was sandwiched between a solid layer of cloud below him and blue sky, criss-crossed by contrails. Now his only contact with the ground was via the radio. 'Leander' came back on the air with the instructions 'Caruso 270. Reconnaissance aircraft. Bird ahead 70'.

Knight's Cross holder Erich Hohagen led III./JG 7 from 9 November 1944 until early 1945, when he was transferred from his post, along with Oberst Steinhoff, on a whim of Reichsmarschall Göring. Hohagen later returned to fly the Me 262 in combat with JV 44 prior to the end of the war. Several sources credit him with at least one victory (whilst others claim he enjoyed no success at all) in the Me 262, adding this to his score of 55 kills with piston-engined aircraft – 11 of which were claimed as early as the Battle of Britain

At a height of 8000 metres, the Me 262 sped towards the target. Buchner scanned his cockpit instruments once more, before receiving another message from 'Leander' which informed him that his distance from the target was decreasing. By this time he had been in the air for well over 20 minutes, and he was still flying above solid cloud. The target was now around ten kilometres away, and Buchner checked his weapons in preparation for the contact. 'Leander' continued to advise him of the closing distance – five kilometres, four kilometres, three kilometres, two kilometres – until he spotted a small dot off to his right which he thought must be the enemy aircraft.

Buchner almost immediately identified the target as a P-38 Lightning (an F-5 reconnaissance variant) and swiftly lined it up in his gunsight, before depressing the trigger on the control column. The first burst of cannon fire was too high, so he dropped the nose a touch and fired the cannons once again . . . and this time hit the target. Flames erupted from the aircraft's starboard wing tank as 30 mm shells smashed into the fuel cell.

The superior speed of the Me 262 soon had Buchner overtaking the stricken Lightning, which rapidly banked to port and fell into a spin. The German pilot manoeuvred his jet into a matching turn, then scanned the sky for the burning Lightning, which had gone spiralling into the cloud layer below – he spotted it just before it entered the cumulus. Buchner then relayed his success to 'Leander' and requested a course for home. The controller offered congratulations in return, and then imparted the course heading 'Caruso 090'. Another check of the instruments – especially those monitoring the efficiency of the temperamental Jumo 004s and the status of their fuel supply – was followed by 'Leander's' instruction that he was to be passed back to 'Bavaria' for the return flight to base. Whilst Buchner had been aloft the weather at Lager-Lechfeld had deteriorated, the cloud base descending to just 500 metres and visibility reducing to 10 to 15 kilometres – he would have to perform a blind landing approach.

As the Me 262 sank into the clouds Buchner's view became decided-

This photo shows Me 262A-1b 'White 3' (Wk-Nr 500071) of 9.*Staffel* III./JG 7. This aircraft entered the annals of Me 262 history whilst being flown by Oberfähnrich Hans-Guido Mutke on the morning of 25 April 1945. The pilot, who had taken off from Fürstenfeldbruck, described his final flight in the aircraft to the author almost 50 years later;

'I made contact with 20 to 25 Marauders north of the Bodensee, then I noticed that I was running very low on fuel while flying over French-occupied territory. I had two choices – to land in Zurich or bale out and use my parachute at 2000 metres. I chose to land in Switzerland as I wanted to avoid being captured by the French, and came down at Zurich's Dübendorf military airfield with only enough fuel left for a further two minutes' flying. The Swiss surrounded the plane with roughly 60 soldiers, all with guns aimed at me – something which struck me as being rather belligerent in neutral Switzerland, particularly since I was 'over the moon' at having escaped being taken prisoner by the French, and had no intention whatsoever of somehow opening fire on the Swiss with my aircraft's weapons.'

Today, Hans-Guido Mutke's aircraft rests in its full glory in the Deutsches Museum in Munich (*via Bundesarchiv*)

Seen at the extreme right of this photo, examining a shrapnel hole in the cowling of his port Jumo 004 turbojet engine, is III./JG 7's Leutnant Hermann Buchner. One of the top four jet aces of World War 2, Buchner destroyed 12 aircraft (most of his kills were against USAAF heavy bombers) with the Me 262, and duly won the Knight's Cross. In mid-April Buchner made his final flight with the Me 262, his jet being bounced by P-51Ds over Steinhuder Lake during an attempted interception of Allied bombers. Buchner succeeded in evading the Mustangs, but whilst on approach for an emergency landing at Rothenburg airfield, he was surprised by an enemy fighter. Still managing to land with his aircraft now on fire, Buchner scrambled out of the cockpit and sprinted away from the jet, before collapsing with shock. In postwar years Buchner reached the rank of Oberst within the Austrian Air Force

ly murky. Speed was held at 650 km/h, and at a height of just 600 metres, the jet broke through the base of the cloud which hung directly over the airfield. Buchner further reduced his speed to 300-250 km/h, lowered the flaps and undercarriage and positioned the fighter for a straight approach. Less than a minute later he felt the main gear compress and heard the reassuring screech of the the tyres as the Me 262 made contact with Lager-Lechfeld's concrete runway – the flight had lasted 80 minutes, from 1135 to 1255. On the same day Major Rudi Sinner also claimed a P-38/F-5 over Lake Ammer.

JG 7'S EX-BOMBER PILOTS

Many of the recruits sent to man JG 7 had been posted in from *Kampfgeschwader*, as former bomber pilots were considered to be ideally qualified to handle the new jet type thanks to their 'C' license rating. A pilot with the latter qualification had had his ability to fly aircraft in excess of 5000 kg in weight officially certified, and been successful in completing contemporary instrument flying courses which allowed him to sortie deep into enemy territory. Bomber pilots could also be expected to effectively lead such long-range missions, whilst simultaneously co-ordinating the individual activities of their crew members. Boasting such recognised skills, an individual that filled these criterion could reasonably be expected to master a jet fighter, and the tactics needed to fly it effectively in combat, in a short space of time. Or could he?

In reality, the highly innovative single-seat Me 262A-1a fighter required its pilot to be not only an excellent flyer, but also an individualist able to spontaneously perform in response to a fluid combat situation – a key strength of the successful *Jagdflieger*. Therefore, the OKL's official strategy of 'streaming' bomber pilots onto the Me 262 because of their perceived technical superiority over their fighter brethren was flawed due to its fundamental failure to take into account their ability to 'fight' the jet in combat. This was quickly proven when a number of experienced *Kampfgeschwader* veterans were

Oberleutnant Hans 'Specker' Grünberg shot down five aircraft (two Lancasters and three B-17s) with the Me 262 whilst flying as a *Staffel* leader with I./JG 7. Grünberg's last few days of the war were spent with JV 44

lost during JG 7's first fighter-v-fighter engagements – the misguided policy was finally abandoned in March 1945.

TRAINING

Conversion training onto the Me 262 was likely to be cursory with the minimum of preparation. For a start, two-seater conversion types were at an absolute premium despite a number of Me 262A-1as having been sent to the Blohm und Voss Wenzendorfer works, on the outskirts of Hamburg, during the autumn of 1944 for modification into dual training types. Only a very small number (believed to be 15) were completed, seven of which were soon written off during training sorties. With few Me 262Bs available, most pilots therefore undertook a conversion course that comprised a ground lecture on the workings of the turbojet, and then a solo flight in the aircraft itself. Gradually, with good fortune and no little skill, the *Jagdflieger* would begin to gain experience of the jet's then unique handling characteristics.

TACTICS

Containing the core of Nowotny's old *Kommando*, it soon became clear that III./JG 7 would be responsible for evolving tactics to be used in combat by the remainder of the *Geschwader*. Considerable debate took place within the *Gruppe* in respect to the best way to use the advantages of the Me 262 (its speed and potent armament) when engaging USAAF four-engined heavy bombers.

III./JG 7 had formed on 19 November 1944, being the first *Gruppe* of the new *Geschwader* to be established – *Kommando Nowotny* had itself been derived from JG 54, KG 1 'Hindenburg' and JG 3 'Udet'. Lager-Lechfeld (the spiritual home of the Me 262) was the location for III./JG 7's rapid assembly under the direct leadership of Major Erich Hohagen who, like Steinhoff, was another veteran fighter ace. Discussion on the appropriate tactics to employ against the heavy bombers as part of the intricate Reich Defence system constantly occupied senior JG 7 pilots, as Steinhoff later recalled;

'We evolved a number of theories as how to best fly the Me 262 against the bomber streams, and were very far from agreement on a common system. Even the experts in this type of engagement were at variance. In practice, we went back to the old conventional attack from behind, approaching the bomber formation – with, of course, tremendous speed – through the defensive fire of the rear gunners and letting off our cannon at short range. The Me 262 was a sensitive and vulnerable piece of machinery, however, and our losses turned out to be higher than we had feared.'

Despite the frenetic activity of the first weeks of the *Geschwader*'s existence, III./JG 7 failed to reach genuine operational status due both to an inadequate supply of new aircraft and replacement parts and an alarming rate of attrition (ten Me 262s lost during the first six weeks) – the result of technical malfunction or pilot error. Things improved with the joint success of Buchner and Sinner at the end of November, but inclement weather during the first three weeks of December severely curtailed both the unit's operational capability and efforts to convert more pilots onto the new fighter.

Hauptmann (later Major) Rudolf Sinner, who took over command of III./JG 7 from Major Erich Hohagen in January 1945. 'Rudi' Sinner is credited with three jet kills in addition to the 37 scored while serving with JGs 27 and 54. Sinner's war ended on 4 April 1945 when he was bounced by P-51s while taking off from Rechlin, the USAAF fighters forcing him to bale out of his stricken machine badly wounded

Throughout this period III./JG 7 was technically involved in defending Berlin from attack by USAAF 'heavies', although its successes were muted. A notable exception occurred on 2 December when Lt Joachim Weber downed three RAF Mosquitos – a feat for which he received the Iron Cross 1st Class, and to which Reichsmarschall Göring is reputed to have exclaimed, 'A fantastic feat with a ship whose engines stop above 6000m and fall apart over 750 kph!'

Following an improvement in the weather at the end of December, JG 7 again commenced operations and conversion training in earnest, and successes in aerial combat against the Allies soon followed.

From July 1944 onwards, Lager-Lechfeld had become a favourite target for both Allied photo-reconnaissance and bomber aircraft. On 23 December III./JG 7's fighters intercepted an F-5 Lightning from the 7th PRG and its escorting P-51Ds from the 353rd FG. In the subsequent action which took place near Magdeburg, Oberfeldwebel Erich Büttner claimed to have shot down a P-51, as did Feldwebel Böckel, yet the 353rd FG reported the loss of just a single aircraft – it is far more likely that the F-5 lost on this sortie was misidentified as a P-51D. Büttner (who was eventually killed in action on 20 March 1945) went on to became one of the first Me 262 aces of the war, claiming at least eight aircraft destroyed.

Formerly an 'old hand' with *Kommando Nowotny*, Büttner had scored his first kills with this pioneering unit on 28 and 29 October, claiming two P-47s and a P-51D. Although he was the first JG 7 ace, Büttner was not the premier jet ace of the war, for this distinction had already been bestowed upon ex-ZG 26 *Zerstörer* pilot Lt Alfred Schreiber, who had achieved five kills by the end of October flying firstly with EKdo 262 and then *Kdo.Nowotny*. Like Büttner, Schreiber

Flugkapitan Karl Baur was Messerschmitt's Chief Test Pilot for experimental aircraft from 1941 to the end of the war. From the summer of 1944 through to May 1945, Baur spent almost all of his time developing the Me 262 – here, he is seen in the cockpit of Me 262 Wk-Nr 130167 in March 1945 evaluating the new EZ 42 automatic gunsight. Baur was unimpressed with this innovation, for he felt that both considerable practice and a radical change in combat tactics was required to ensure that maximum effectiveness was derived from the gunsight. Despite Baur's caution, several of JG 7's jets were equipped with the EZ 42, and one of its few successes was achieved by Unteroffizier Geisthovel on 8 April 1945 when he claimed two P-51Ds destroyed

The two photos on this spread show unguided R4M ('M' referring to the explosive head) air-to-air rockets fitted neatly below the wing of a JG 7 Me 262A-1a. These weapons were first used in combat by the *Geschwader* on 18 March 1945, roughly 60 Me 262A-1as being equipped with the rockets (12 rounds beneath each wing) on this day – a further six jets received the 24-round fitment. Pilots reported that the results achieved with the R4Ms were devastating

also failed to survive the war, being killed in a collision with a Spitfire on 26 November 1944.

Few 'heavies' were claimed in these early actions, however, a fact which seems to have confirmed 'Macki' Steinhoff's concerns surrounding the Me 262's ability to engage bomber formations. He had always believed that the jet's real strength lay in tackling the escorts, leaving the *Jagdwaffe*'s piston-engined fighters free to then press home their attacks on undefended bombers. It was also clear that inexperienced pilots were finding the jet almost impossible to master. Having voiced these opinions to senior Luftwaffe commanders, Steinhoff and Hohagen (both outspoken individuals) were viewed by Göring as dissenters who were impeding Hitler's order that the Me 262 was to be used exclusively to attack bombers, engaging fighters 'only in passing'.

Göring vented his wrath at Adolf Galland, *General der Jagdflieger*, who in turn, on a wet morning at the aerodrome of Parchim, expressed his frustration to Steinhoff at the latter's apparent tardiness in making JG 7 an effective fighter unit. It was clear to Steinhoff that Göring was looking to replace him with a 'younger, more positive, man'.

Galland and Steinhoff had planned a co-ordinated attack against the heavy bombers early in the New Year, yet it was whilst the latter was away looking for appropriate forward airfields that he received the news that he had been replaced as *Kommodore* of JG 7 by 30-year-old Major Theodor Weissenberger, until then *Kommandeur* of I./JG 7. Major Hohagen, Steinhoff's able *Kommandeur* of III./JG 7, was also dismissed to make way for Major Rudolf Sinner – like their predecessors, both Weissenberger and Sinner were veteran fighter aces. Despite being removed from JG 7, Steinhoff and Hohagen would later reappear as Me 262 pilots within JV 44 during the last weeks of the war.

Göring immediately ordered Weissenberger and Sinner to raise JG 7 to its full strength within 15 days of their appointments. Following intensive flying training, considerable co-operation from the ground controllers and the implementation of new flying control equipment, the *Geschwader* rapidly improved its operational capability. However, on New Year's Day JG 7 lost two aircraft in separate incidents.

Leutnant Heinrich Lönnecker was flying his 9th *Staffel* Me 262A-1a (Wk-Nr 500021) in support of the piston-engined fighters of JG 301, and his former unit JG 300, when his aircraft was bounced by a P-51D flown by Lt Franklin Young of the 336th FS/4th FG. Lönnecker was killed in the attack, which occurred to the west of Fassburg. The second Me 262 written off on 1 January 1945 was being flown by II./JG 7's Hellmut Detjens, who had to force-land Wk-Nr 500039 due to an engine failure. The recounting of his story gives ample evidence of the traumatic life of the Me 262 pilot during these harrowing times;

'Our squadron flight controller, Lt Preusker (who later became a Minister within the Department of Housing!), reported the approach of an enemy reconnaissance aircraft over the Ostsee (the Baltic Sea). Lt Weber and I took off as a *Rotte*, and were directed by Preusker. I was at full power, but Weber started to pull away from me, and when I asked him to power back he just sped on and vanished into the distance.

'In the hope of still catching a Lightning or Mosquito unawares, I kept to my present course. Then suddenly one of my engines lost power and flamed out. The only thing I knew was that I was quite high and somewhere over the Ostsee. Below me, the clouds had closed up to form a solid, impenetrable, blanket. I called control over the radio, turned the aircraft onto a reverse heading, then started to call my field, which was Brandenburg, using code "077", but received no answer. I then tried to establish contact with Lärz, Burg and finally Oranienburg – no response. I heard nothing, only the wind rushing past my cockpit and the roar of my one remaining engine.

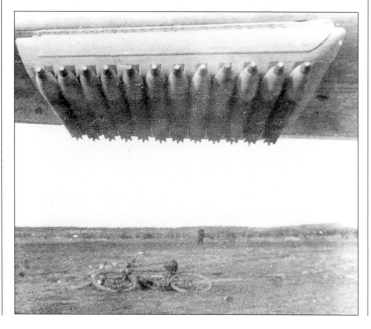

A standard battery fitment of 12 R4Ms on an underwing launch rail had little detrimental effect on the airflow over the wing of the Me 262

A fine portrait of 11./JG 7's youthful Hellmut Detjens, and his pet, taken in September 1944 (*via Hellmut Detjens*)

III./JG 7 pilot Leutnant Victor Petermann was credited with the destruction of a B-17G on 22 March 1945 and a second Flying Fortress eight days later. A veteran of 550 operational sorties, Petermann finished the war with 64 kills, all bar two of which had been scored with JG 52 on the Russian front

'Time passed me by and I tried not to think of the possible disaster awaiting me. I called on the radio again and said that the second engine was faltering. I'd no sooner said that when it died on me. At nearly the same time I heard over my headphones "077 Brandenburg calling". I started counting so that the piling (radar) operator could get a fix on my position, and pushed the stick forward. I saw the solid mass of clouds rush towards me, and the piling operator came on the radio again. "Can hardly get a fix on you. Your position must be very close to the field – will fire flares". I pulled back the stick a bit, levelled out the aircraft, saw an opening in the clouds and pushed on through them. I pressed the speak button on the radio again and told control, "This is not Brandenburg. I will belly-land".

'Beneath me I saw woods and snowy fields, and in the distance yellow-brown sand. What I'd learned in the past was now put to instinctive use – that is "don't dither about when you have chosen where to land, and under no circumstances change your approach". I flew on towards my goal, gaining more speed, which took me over the trees, and then I saw my chosen landing area which, to my disgust, was not level at all but covered in craters and small hillocks. I re-tightened my seat webbing, got rid of my cockpit cover, then suddenly to the right of me near a house I saw a flash and a mushroom cloud of smoke. Too late to pull up and too late to leave the aircraft, I concentrated on the landing.

'I followed the contours of the ground and felt the aircraft's speed drop away. Then, near an almost level slope, I gently let the engines touch the ground. But then, at the highest part of the slope, I saw a crater which I hit, ripping off my engine, sliding 20 or 30 metres before I came to a stop. I breathed a sigh of relief, undid the seat harness and took off my flying helmet. A whistling noise made me jump out of the cockpit and I ended up flat on the ground. I then felt a tremendous pressure wave rolling over me and I immediately thought that I was under attack by enemy aircraft fire, but could not hear any engine noise. After a while another whistling sound made me dive into a nearby depression. I felt the waves of this second depression wash over me and saw, in the distance, a fountain of smoke shoot up, followed by complete silence again.

'I sprinted towards the house which I had seen on my landing approach, as it now lay directly in front of me, approximately 1000 metres away. Between the house and myself the ground was covered with shell-holes and craters – a proper moonscape. Upon reaching the house, it revealed itself to be a camouflaged bunker. My frantic banging on the iron door was greeted with complete indifference from the presumed occupants. I picked up a stone and banged the door again, this time obtaining the desired result. A feldwebel opened the door. He looked me up and down as I stood in my leather flying gear and said "What do you want?" I told him "I've just landed here". He seemed unable to comprehend my answer, retorting "This is not an airfield".

'The officer in charge duly told me that my emergency "silver" landing field was, in fact, and artillery testing ground where they had just been evaluating compressed air grenades as I landed! After the firing had ceased, I was taken by the operations officer on a motor-bike combination to my aircraft so I could pick up my parachute and radio. It was not a serious crash, and by the look of the aircraft only a few R4M rockets had broken away from their moorings and were hanging down from under the wing, thus presenting an intimidating sight – this probably explains why the two guards posted to watch the aircraft kept a respectful distance.

'We took the motor bike combination and drove to Jüterbog, where I was to make arrangements for the aircraft to be picked up. I eventually reached the airfield at Brandenburg-Briest before midnight.'

Detjens' account illustrates that technical problems, lack of replacement parts, crashes caused by pilot error and, inevitably, the foul winter weather (often fog so thick that it was difficult to see more than a couple of metres in any direction) continued to plague the operations of JG 7. This was never more apparent than at the base at Kaltenkirchen, in Holstein, which had been specifically chosen to allow Me 262s to operate in the northern air defence of Bremen, Hamburg and Lübeck, and also to povide a protective barrier against incoming USAAF bombers making their way down to Berlin.

Kaltenkirchen was to be the first 'real' home of I./JG 7, commanded by one the Luftwaffe's greatest aces, Major Erich Rudorffer, who had scored over 200 victories. The *Gruppe* began to prepare for its impending operational status from 8 January 1945 onwards, Rudorffer having been appointed to command I./JG 7 in place of the promoted Weissenberger. Under the leadership of the latter individual, the *Gruppe* had made abortive attempts to become operational, but had been continually dogged by a gross lack of equipment. Indeed, it was not until mid-February that progress began to be made at Kaltenkirchen.

Each of the three *Staffeln* that comprised I./JG 7 was led by a top ace, namely Oberleutnants Hans-Peter Waldmann, Hans 'Specker' Grünberg and Fritz Stehle – both Waldmann and Grünberg already wore the Knight's Cross. Stehle and Grünberg survived the war, but Waldmann was killed on 18 March 1945 – his final sortie is detailed later in this chapter.

Although January 1945 saw JG 7 enjoy some success whilst continuing to focus on conversion training, endless problems with the Me 262's temperamental Jumo 004 engines, and the consequential loss of aircraft and pilots, provided a less than positive start to the New Year. Indeed, I./JG 7's first fatality of 1945 was caused by technical failure, Unteroffizier Hans Werner suffering engine failure on a maintenance flight and crashing near Alveslohe. During February, however, some of the leading jet aces finally began to make names for themsleves.

Things did not look promising at the start of the month though, as a continual low cloud base over the airfields at Brandenburg-Briest, Parchim and Oranienburg severely affected JG 7's operational combat capacity. Despite the poor weather, the first days of February saw a new ace enjoy his first successes with the Me 262 – Lt Rudolf 'Rudi' Rademacher of III./JG 7 would end the war as one of the highest scoring jet aces of the conflict. His career is worth a closer look.

Like many Me 262 pilots, Rademacher was already a successful *Experte* by the time he came to fly the jet, having achieved 81 victories with I. and III./JG 54 – this tally included an incredible haul of seven kills on 5 July 1943 alone. Immediately prior to flying the Me 262, Rudi Rademacher had served as an instructor with 1./Erg.Gr (*Ergänzungsgruppe Nord*) at Sagan, where, despite his training duties, he had still managed to shoot down five USAAF aircraft! Awarded the Knight's Cross for his actions on the Russian Front, Rademacher flew the Me 262 for the first time on 30 January 1945, and effectively completed his conversion training just two days later when he scored his premier combat victory with the jet whilst flying with the 11th *Staffel* of III./JG 7.

Directed by fighter control towards a photo-reconnaissance Spitfire flying at 11,000 m above Braunschweig, Rademacher's approach was masked from the RAF pilot the condensation trail left by the latter's aircraft. Moving to a slightly higher position whilst still unseen, the *Jagdflieger* opened fire with his quartet of 30 mm cannon. Caught totally by surprise, the defenceless Spitfire took the full force of Rademacher's well aimed burst and plummeted to the ground. Just two days later he claimed a B-17 out of a formation of USAAF bombers attacking Magdeburg. On 9 February (the first operation for III./JG 7 in six days after a spell of inclement weather) Rademacher claimed two B-17s over Berlin, this sortie also seeing high-scoring Me 262 aces Oberleutnant Günther Wegmann, Hauptmann Georg-Peter Eder and Lt Karl Schnörrer all enjoying success.

On St Valentine's Day Rademacher claimed a B-17 en route to Neumünster, and 48 hours later he continued his destructive sequence

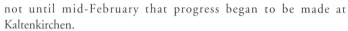

This photo of jet ace Leutnant 'Hadi' Weihs was taken shortly after he had destroyed a P-51D over Berlin on 9 April 1945 (*via 'Hadi' Weihs*)

by downing his first American fighter in the form of a P-51D. Eight days later he destroyed yet another B-17, quickly followed by a B-24, during attacks on Halle and Leipzig. In the month of February alone, Rademacher scored at least seven jet kills according to some historians .

Continuing to his run of success throughout the months of March and April, he was finally credited with at least 16 kills – including several 'Herausschuss' ('shooting out') claims – in lists published in the early postwar years, but more recent works on JG 7 have revised his tally down to 8 victories.

The 'Herausschuss' tactic (as opposed to 'shooting down') acknowledged a pilot's skill in removing an enemy bomber from the collective protection of its formation, and was employed effectively by Me 262 pilots, who exploited the fighter's superior speed and rate of climb. If all went to plan, the stricken bomber would fall out of formation, thus making it easy prey for other marauding Luftwaffe fighters who would move in for the kill.

Throughout his career, Rademacher flew over 500 operational sorties, claiming 102 victories. He survived the war, but like his great jet ace contemporaries Heinz Bär, Kurt Welter and Theodore Weissenberger, Knight's Cross holder Rademacher was killed in a glider accident close to his birth place of Luneburg on 13 June 1953.

Despite the success (albeit somewhat isolated) of men like Rademacher, one by one the early jet pilots from the previous autumn continued to fall, thus robbing the Me 262 force of its most experienced *Jagdflieger*. On 21 February 1945 10./JG 7 pilot Oberfeldwebel Helmut Baudach (one of the original members of EKdo 262) baled out over Schönwalde/Niederbayern after his aircraft was severely hit by enemy gunfire, injuring the pilot in the process. As he left the cockpit, Baudach's head struck the jet's tailplane, and although he managed to land safely, he succumbed to his injuries just a few days later.

On the same day another top Luftwaffe ace in the form of Oberleutnant Hans-Peter Waldmann (leader of 9./JG 7) claimed a P-51D at 1202 and another at 1217 as his *Rotte* joined the action against the overwhelming Allied force of 3000+ aircraft which was operating as air cover in support of Operation *Clarion*.

Throughout this period of intense activity, other JG 7 pilots had been steadily building scores as familiarity with the Me 262 grew. Pre-war Luftwaffe fighter pilot Georg-Peter Eder had seen action both during the Battle of Britain and on the opening day of Operation *Barbarossa*, and he was eventually awarded the Knight's Cross in June 1944. Three months later, on 27 September, Eder was given command of III./EJG 2, which had been derived from component parts of the experimental jet unit EKdo 262.

On 8 November, Eder was standing alongside Generalleutnant Galland on the airfield at Achmer, south of Osnabruck, when they witnessed the death of Major Walter Nowotny. As detailed in the previous chapter, Galland immediately appointed Eder to take over Nowotny's mantle, and just under three weeks later he was decorated with the Oakleaves to the Knight's Cross – this coveted decoration was awarded to him 72 hours after he had destroyed three B-17s in a single combat. A courageous and daring practitioner of his trade, Eder has

When Oberleutnant Walter Schuck was made *Staffelkapitan* of 3./JG 7 on 24 March 1945 he had already scored 198 kills with JG 5 flying Fw 190s on the Eismeer Front, in Scandinavia. He quickly mastered the Me 262, shooting down eight aircraft in the final weeks of the conflict, including two P-51Ds on his first sortie as *Staffelkapitan* on 24 March, and four B-17Gs on 10 April – Schuck, himself, was shot down in the latter sortie, although he managed to bale out safely

been credited with pioneering Luftwaffe head-on attacks against enemy bomber formations – he was shot down on no less than 17 occasions and wounded 14 times. Eder also proved himself to be an effective ground attack pilot with the jet, and during the Ardennes offensive of late 1944 he claimed to have destroyed some 40 P-47s on the ground. Indeed, Thunderbolts (and B-17s) seem to have been Eder's favoured prey, for whilst serving as *Staffelkapitän* of 9./JG 7, he continued to knock down singles and pairs of these aircraft through to April 1945.

In fact Eder gained the distinction of being the last Luftwaffe pilot to down a Flying Fortress of the 1st Air Division when he destroyed B-17G *The Towering Titan* of the 305th BG south of Berlin on 17 April. It is reputed that the German pilot had gained a reputation with USAAF (and previously RAF) bomber crews for affording them time to bale out of stricken aircraft, prior to moving in for the kill. Shot down and hospitalised by the end of the war, Eder eventually pursued a successful career in business before finally passing away in 1986.

JG 7's operations prior to the final nine weeks of war largely saw the *Geschwader* sending small numbers of jets in *Rotte* or *Schwarm* formations aloft to meet the enemy on the outskirts of Berlin. Moving into March 1945, its strategy shifted significantly as large numbers of Me 262s were simultaneously ordered into action. This new ethos was put into practice for the first time on 3 March when all available aircraft from the *Geschwaderstab* and III./JG 7 (a total of some 29 jets) took of from Oranienburg, Brandenburg-Briest and Parchim.

At 1015 the large formation of jets engaged B-17s and B-24s, and escorting fighters, sent to bomb Magdeburg. Between this city and Braunschweig, 9./JG 7 – the *Staffel* from Parchim, which included such notable jet pilots as Buchner, Gutmann, Schnörrer and Wegmann – wreaked havoc. Opposed by a veritable wall of defensive fire, it was inevitable that not all the *Jagdflieger* would survive the attack unscathed, and Hauptmann Heinz Gutmann was duly killed when the cockpit of his Me 262A-1 (Wk-Nr 110558) was hit by enemy fire, causing him to dive into the ground. Although Gutmann scored just two kills with the jet prior to his death, his skill as one of Germany's finest bomber pilots had been recognised with the award of the Knight's Cross in April of the previous year.

Pilots from *Stab.*, 10. and 11./JG 7 had also enjoyed success on 3 March, with Major 'Rudi' Sinner and long-standing jet pilot Helmut Lennartz claiming at least one kill apiece. The USAAF admitted losses of six bombers and three fighters.

March was also the month that JG 7 first used R4M air-to-air rockets, which replaced the expensive (and therefore rare) wire-guided Ruhrstahl X-4s. Initially tested at Rechlin during 1944, the R4M was first used operationally on the 18th of the month when a dozen 4 kg rockets were fitted to some 54 jets – a further 6 aircraft from 9.*Staffel* received a 24-shot fitment. The reported effects of the new weapon were startling, for bombers were literally blown apart on contact. With the advent of rockets, it became difficult for *Jagdflieger* to determine the numbers of aircraft destroyed, or indeed which kills were to be credited to individual Luftwaffe pilots. The result was that credits on this day were made as group kills, not on an individual basis. A total of

13 kills were credited to JG 7 for the loss of three pilots and five jets.

One of the trio of men downed during this action was veteran jet ace Oberleutnant Günther Wegmann, who was replaced as *Staffelkapitän* of 9./JG 7 by Lt Karl Schnörrer. Wegmann later described his final action from his hospital bed, explaining that over Glöwen he had opened fire on a B-17. As his shells struck the wings of the heavy bomber, so his own canopy was shattered by return fire. Wegmann felt a heavy impact on his right leg and, after pulling away from the attack, he had used his hand to inspect the wound, which was gaping, but not causing him undue discomfort.

As the aircraft still seemed to be flyable, Wegmann decided to attempt a landing at Parchim, but at a height of 4000 m the right tur-bojet flamed out, and he took to his parachute. Fortunate to survive the low altitude bale-out, the oberleutnant had had his wounds initial-ly treated by a Red Cross sister, but a few hours later his right leg was amputated in hospital.

The haemorrhaging of aces on the 18th continued later that day when JG 7 lost one of its finest pilots, Oberleutnant Hans-Peter Waldmann. Just 23 years old at the time of his death, 'Dackel' Waldmann had joined the Luftwaffe in 1940, but did not enter com-bat until August 1942 over the Russian Front. Flying with JG 52, he rose to the rank of *Staffelkapitän* and received the Knight's Cross fol-lowing his 85th victory in February 1944. His final tally in the east was 125 kills.

Waldmann (and his *Staffel*) was transferred to JG 3 in response to the Normandy invasion on 6 June 1944, and once in France, he con-tinued to score freely. By the time his *Staffel* had been posted to Lager-Lechfeld for conversion onto the Me 262 in December 1944,

This postwar shot shows the tail of Oberfeldwebel Heinz Arnold's Me 262A-1a Wk-Nr 500491. Whilst flying this fighter with 11./JG 7, he scored seven victories (to add to his 42 pis-ton-engined kills) between 3 and 24 March 1945. Arnold's run of success ended on 17 April when he was lost during a ground attack sortie whilst flying another jet – 500491 was undergoing maintenance at Alt Lönnewitz at the time. The aircraft was then taken over by Leutnant Fritz Müller, who flew it from Prague-Ruzyn to Lechfeld in order to surrender to US troops on 8 May 1945 (*via NASM*)

Waldmann had taken his tally to 132. His was one of three *Staffeln* to comprise I./JG 7, the others being led by Oberleutnants Stehle and Grünberg, all under the command of Major Weissenberger. Waldmann went into action with the Me 262 for the first time on 22 February 1945 when, as reported earlier, he shot down two P-51Ds. The nomination for the Oak Leaves to his Knight's Cross followed, but in the event this was to be awarded posthumously. His death on 18 March 1945 whilst at the controls of Me 262A-1 Wk-Nr 117097 'Yellow 3' was recounted in 1992 to the author by Waldmann's colleague on that final flight, Leutnant Hans-Dieter 'Hadi' Weihs;

'The weather over Kaltenkirchen was very bad – low, hanging, clouds with poor visibility. The end of the runway was shrouded in mist, and we were told that the cloud ceiling was at 6000 m. No improvement was expected. Our CO, Major Erich Rudorffer, took the opportunity to drive over to Divisional Operations. This was the day when we were expecting a large attack of American aircraft against Berlin – 2000 aircraft in all, 1300 of which were bombers.

'It was then that the duty operations officer (I think it was the leader of our first flight, Oberleutnant Grünberg) received a phone call from Göring, who was shouting so loud down the phone that even the personnel in the operations room could hear him. He ordered us to take-off immediately. He swore at us, and ended his tirade of abuse with the expression "Die Kalten Heinis", which, when politely translated, means "a bunch of old women".

'We started with four aircraft per flight, three flights in all. As I was the only pilot with instrument flying experience, I was to lead the flight. In order to lead my little "Schwarm" through the many layers of heavy cloud, it had been decided beforehand that we were to fly in a very tight formation, wing-tip to wing-tip, with me in the centre and the other three aircraft bunched around me. To my right was my "*Rotten*" leader, Oberfahnrich Schrey, whilst to the left was the flight leader, Hans-Peter Waldmann, and next to him was his "*Rotten*" leader, Oberfeldwebel Gerhard Reiher. As we were about to take-off, Reiher's plane came to a stop with a damaged turbine, and we were left with three aircraft.

'We formed a tight formation, and flew in a big loop into the low-hanging cloud. At a height of about 700 m, Waldmann went missing and only Schrey remained with me. We had arranged that if anyone missed the link up, both Waldmann and Schrey would fly to my left (as seen from my viewpoint). Then, at about 800 metres, directly over the forest of Saxony, there was an almighty bang underneath and behind me. Waldmann had come up through the clouds and, unable to see me, rammed my aircraft. Left in a flat spin, I scrambled out of the cockpit and onto the wing in order to parachute to the ground.

'We felt quite "windy" about jumping out over the forest of Sachsen as it was studded with ancient trees, the branches of which were like spears. I was lucky and landed on a small lawn next to the station-master's house near the Hamburg-Berlin railway line, which even then was electrified! Soon after, I heard the explosion of my aircraft hitting the ground, followed by Waldmann's plane. Then I heard the sound of gun fire. I looked up to see that it was directed at Oberfähnrich Schrey, who had had the misfortune to break through the clouds in front of a formation of American P-51s, who promptly shot him down. Schrey parachuted out of his stricken craft, and was dangling at the end of his 'chute when he was again fired on by the enemy and killed. This was concluded to have been the cause of his death by a board of enquiry.

'After I had landed I gave orders to the forestry commission at Schwarzenbek that members of the Volkssturm were to look for Waldmann, who had parachuted out of his Me 262. Eventually he was found quite a long way from his crashed aircraft, lying peacefully on his face, with only the top of his head torn open. Waldmann and Schrey were buried with full military honours at Kaltenkirchen.'

This account by 'Hadi' Weihs (who was the only survivor from the three who took to the air that morning in Kaltenkirchen) is most valuable for it disproves other versions of Waldmann's final moments. Weihs himself was a highly experienced pilot, having joined the Luftwaffe in 1936, and he duly replaced Waldmann as *Staffelkapitän* of 3./JG 7. He eventually became one of the key Me 262 aces of the war, surviving the conflict with eight jet kills to his credit.

Another leading JG 7 ace who started scoring kills with the Me 262 in March was III.*Gruppe Jagdflieger* Leutnant Alfred Ambs (he would finish with a tally of seven victories), who today is the secretary for all units associated with the jet. On the 14th Ambs, together with Leutnant Joachim Weber and Unteroffizier Giefing, took off from Brandenburg-Briest to intercept enemy reconnaissance aircraft. Ambs later recalled that after 20 minutes, they spotted two P-51Ds (probably F-6 recce variants) flying on a westerly course. Weber opened fire out of range, which alerted the USAAF pilots to the impending attack and allowed them to take evasive action.

The trio of jets then broke away from the Mustangs in a deliberate attempt to persuade them that the attack was over. However, the Me 262s then made a second pass, but this time from head-on. With a closing speed of 1400 kph, Ambs fired his cannons from about 300 m. He recalled, 'The P-51 flying in the lead position exploded into a thousand pieces'. The second fighter also fell, this time to Weber's fire.

Continuing to operate in greater strength, JG 7 scrambled its entire III.*Gruppe* force on the 19th to meet incoming B-17s from the 3rd Air Division north of Chemnitz. Although only 28 Me 262s actually made contact with the enemy, at least four 'heavies' were destroyed by R4M rockets. The following day 22 jets intercepted bombers, and escorting fighters, in the Hamburg area and downed nine B-17s for the loss of four jets. This pattern continued for the rest of the month.

However, fuel rationing, which had all but crippled the Luftwaffe's conventional fighter force since the end of 1944, now began to hit JG 7. As reserves of the high octane fuel required for the Me 262's twin turbojets rapidly dwindled, operations became so seriously affected that the USAAF began to progressively target 'Silber' (Me 262) bases with relative impunity. Jet production sites and training airfields were also hit, all of which combined to gradually reduce the deadly threat posed by the virtually unstoppable Me 262.

The potency of the Messerschmitt fighter had been graphically demonstrated in a five-day period between 18-22 March when Me 262 pilots were credited with the destruction of at least 50 enemy aircraft. This success seemed to regenerate enthusiasm for the jet from the political hierarchy, and Hitler once again began to extol the virtues of the Me 262 as a war winning machine, congratulating its units on their recent successes and instructing that armament should be improved.

Over the next two weeks Major Heinrich Ehrler (another of the Luftwaffe's highest scoring fighter pilots) began to amass his jet score whilst flying as part of the *Geschwaderstab* of JG 7. Something of an enigma, Erhler had enjoyed great success as commander of III./JG 5 (based in Scandinavia), scoring 201 kills, for which he was decorated with the Oak Leaves to the Knight's Cross. However, in late 1944 he was court-martialled because his unit had failed to provide aerial defence for the battleship *Tirpitz*, moored in a nearby Norwegian fjord, during a raid which had seen it attacked and sunk by RAF Lancasters on 12 November 1944. Over 1000 German sailors had lost their lives when the vessel capsized.

A court-martial produced evidence that Ehrler's unit had failed to respond to radio messages from the ship requesting immediate air support. Sentenced to death, the major was only reprieved because of his previously exemplary combat record, and by the *Jagdwaffe's* desperate need for experienced men to fly Me 262s. Like many other veteran piston-engined *Jagdflieger*, Ehrler quickly got to grips with the jet, downing a B-17 on 21 March, a second Flying Fortress 24 hours later and a third on 24 March. On the last day of the month Ehrler removed a P-51D from an escorting formation, claiming a '*Herausschuss*'.

His final sortie on 6 April saw him in action near Schaarlippe, where he was observed to destroy a further pair of B-17s before Ehrler himself was shot down and killed by P-51s. He was buried in the cemetery at Stendal on 10 April. Major Heinrich Ehrler had flown in the region of

Close up photo of the kill markings on Oberfeldwebel Heinz Arnold's Me 262A-1a. The number 42 signifies his earlier successes, whilst each of the star-topped bars denote his subsequent jet victories. Today, Wk-Nr 500491 rests within the US National Air and Space Museum in Washington DC, having been meticulously restored (over 6000 hours were spent on the refurbishment) in 1978-79

400 operational sorties during the war, with his final score of 206 kills giving him one of the best 'strike rates' of any Luftwaffe pilot.

The threat posed to the Allied heavy bomber force by JG 7 reached its zenith on 31 March 1945. Flying aircraft equipped with R4M rockets and MK 108 explosive shells, both I. and III. *Gruppen* took part in four separate combats thoughout the day aimed at repelling not USAAF daylight bombers, but RAF Lancasters and Halifaxes. Although Bremen, Wilhelmshaven and Hamburg were their targets, the British 'heavies' themselves soon became vulnerable to the high speed slashing attacks of the Me 262s.

Throughout the day, some 21 bombers were destroyed by the jets, and many more returned to their bases heavily damaged. Direct hits from the rockets often caused horrendous explosions, and an inexplicable lack of fighter cover accentuated the ease with which the Me 262s got amongst the bombers. A number of JG 7 pilots recorded single kills, whilst Grünberg, Sturm, Todt, Schenk, Schall and Ehrig all claimed two enemy aircraft destroyed apiece. Hadi Weihs and Gerhard Reiher also added to their scores.

Despite this success, I./JG 7 was ordered to evacuate Kalternkirchen the following day, 1. *Staffel* being instructed to move to Bradenburg-Briest, 2. *Staffel* to Burg and 3. *Staffel* to Oranienburg. Just three days later its *Kommandeur*, Major Erich Rudorffer, was transferred away from the *Gruppe*, leaving each *Staffel* to operate chiefly as autonomous units, independent of the *Geschwader*, until the final fortnight of war. Whilst March had shown JG 7 to be *the* definitive jet fighter operator of World War 2, it had also been the month in which several of the *Geschwader's* most experienced fighter pilots had been lost, and its operational strength reduced to well below 60 jets.

On 1 April seven USAAF bombers fell to JG 7's firepower, but at Parchim three days later disaster struck when 15 Me 262s were caught by American fighters at their most vulnerable point in a combat sortie – on take-off. Ponderous when launching (and indeed upon their return to base when approaching to landing), the Me 262s were usually covered by 'flak lanes' specially arranged to ensure some protection until the Jumo 004 turbojets reached efficient, high speed, revolutions. With P-51Ds already over the base as the Me 262s took off and made for cloud in an attempt to mask their efforts at gaining height, 504th FS/339th FG fighter pilot Robert Havighurst describes what happenned next;

'We spotted three Me 262s climbing through a gap in the cloud. We let them come nearer, losing altitude all the while. When the first Me 262 was in range I opened fire from above and behind. The German tried to shake me off in a descending left turn. Thanks to my greater speed I was able to stay with him easily and scored hits on his left wing. Suddenly I came under heavy anti-aircraft fire. I released my drop tanks and began evasive manoeuvres to escape the flak. The Me 262 used this brief period to begin climbing again. However, I was able to quickly get behind him again and began to fire once more. I observed hits on his forward fuselage and left wing. At about 600 m the Me 262 suddenly went into a dive. I saw no parachute. I suspect the pilot was killed by a hit on the cockpit.'

The flight leader on this fateful morning was Rudi Sinner, who, despite his great experience and skill with the aircraft, was totally overwhelmed when set up by four P-51Ds. Sinner's aircraft was quickly hit, and as the Me 262 was close to the ground, he decided to bale out immediately after performing an evasive manoeuvre. After a precarious decent by parachute, Sinner landed in a ploughed field, where he later reported that he had been strafed by the Mustangs. Feigning death by lying prone on the ground, Sinner survived one attacking pass before running to find cover in a furrow.

Daylight bomber formations continued to attack and severely damage the Me 262 'Silber' bases, further reducing the operational capability of the rapidly decreasing number of jets. J-2 fuel for the Jumo 004s was also becoming progressively more scarce as the days went by. By mid-April, various *Staffeln* of JG 7 had been transferred to bases in Bavaria and Czechoslovakia, and at this point the command structure for the *Geschwader* becomes confused. Already psychologically and physically challenged, JG 7's pilots were now also devoid of any real leadership.

Frequent strafing attacks by Allied fighters continued to make the airfields vulnerable – worse still for those Me 262s caught taking off or returning to base, as was seen on 17 April at Saaz when P-47s and P-51s discovered a *Schwarm* of Me 262s, led by Oberleutnant Grünberg, about to land. The jets had no chance against the overwhelming number of predatory USAAF fighters, and all four were shot down. Only Grünberg parachuted to safety. Jet victories continued to be scored, but without ever achieving anywhere near the level of success enjoyed by JG 7 during late March.

Several combats with Soviet VVS aircraft occurred during the final weeks of the war, and whilst the Me 262 met impressive foes in the La-5, -7 and -9 and the Yak-3, -7 and -9, even the renowned resilience of the much slower Il-2 *Sturmovik* ground attack aircraft failed to save it from destruction by the Luftwaffe jet.

On 30 April, JG 7 pilot Lt Fritz Kelb (the sole *Jagdflieger* to have achieved kills on both the Me 163 and Me 262) was killed in action. Following Hitler's death on that same day, new bases were identified for JG 7's jets. Indeed, instructions were issued at around the same time that IV./JG 7 was to be formed out of JV 44! It was not until the final day of the war in Europe that JG 7 surrendered its final 15 jets to the victorious Allies. The final postscript to this brief history of the world's first jet fighter unit should rest with General Adolf Galland, one of the greatest protagonists for the use of the Me 262 as Germany's *sole* frontline fighter;

'I am of the opinion that with only 300 Messerschmitt Me 262 jet fighters we could have on any day shot down a minimum of 200 bombers. If this would have continued for a week or two, then the day bombing would have had to be stopped. As a consequence, the dimensions of the destruction of the targets in Germany would have been diminished. As a negative consequence, the war would have been prolonged, and the Russians allowed more time to conquer further German territory. So let us now be satisfied with Hitler's mistakes towards the legendary Messerschmitt Me 262.'

THE FINAL EFFORT

Back in November 1944 (just over two weeks prior to the activation of JG 7) yet another experimental *Kommando* had been established. Its task was to evaluate the Me 262's potential as a nightfighter – more specifically as an 'anti-Mosquito' aircraft. Able to go about their lethal business in the night skies of Germany virtually unchallenged, these fast high-altitude intruders were an ever growing menace. Several *Staffeln* of single-engined fighters had already been set up to combat them, but they had enjoyed limited success. It was hoped the Me 262's superior speed would provide the answer.

Not surprisingly perhaps, the officer selected to head the new *Kommando* was one of the more successful of the single-engined exponents. Up until a year earlier, Leutnant Kurt Welter had been a flying instructor, but his transfer to the nocturnal defence of the Reich was to demonstrate where his real abilities lay – in September 1944 he was responsible for no less than three of the seven Mosquitos brought down. The following month he was awarded the Knight's Cross for having achieved 33 kills (5 by day) in just 40 missions. And on 2 November 1944 the *Kommando Welter* (what else?) was activated at Burg, near Magdeburg, with a complement of two Me 262 single-seaters, one of which had been equipped with FuG 226 'Neuling' IFF.

Initially, however, Welter operated out of Rechlin-Lärz, patrolling the Berlin area on '*helle Nachtjagd*' (visual nightfighting) sorties in con-

Completed Me 262s coming off the assembly line of the heavily camouflaged factory at Laupheim, south of Ulm. Messerschmitt continued to produce large numbers of the twin-engined jet during the early months of 1945, and although accepted by the Luftwaffe, relatively few of them actually saw combat with frontline units

The enigmatic Oberleutnant Kurt Welter was quite probably the highest scoring Me 262 pilot of all time. As commanding officer of *Kommando Welter* (10./NJG 11), which was the sole Me 262 night-fighting unit, Welter claimed 25 Mosquitos and two four-engined heavy bomber with the jet – he has been widely credited with 20+ jet victories, his final overall tally being 63. Although he survived the war, Welter was killed in a car accident on 7 March 1949

Me 262A-1a of III./EJG 2 is seen taxyingbehind a stationary 'White 3' at Lager-Lechfeld in October 1944. Although flying almost exclusively during daylight hours, this *Gruppe* was also charged with training the handful of jet nightfighter pilots posted to 10./NJG 11

junction with the capital's flak and searchlight defences. He claimed a number of kills in this manner, and if a congratulatory signal from the GOC *I.Jagdkorps* addressed to Rechlin and dated 28 November is anything to go by, the first nocturnal victory achieved by an Me 262 may well have been a Mosquito shot down the night before.

Oberleutnant Welter added a Lancaster to his growing list of Mosquitos on the night of 12/13 December 1944, and by the New Year his small *Kommando* was beginning to grow in numbers as one or two new aircraft arrived. With the backing of higher authority, he trawled the nightfighter arm for suitable pilots to fly them. On 21 January 1945 the unit sustained its first fatality, however, when Oberleutnant Heinz Bruckmann was killed attempting an emergency landing on open heathland near Wittstock, north-west of Berlin. And on 4 February two further pilots were lost in crashes, one during a transfer flight and the other while training.

The end of February saw the unit, which had been subordinated to NJG 11 for administrative purposes since its inception, officially redesignated as 10./NJG 11, although the members continued to refer to themselves as the *Kommando Welter*. It was at this time, too, that their strength reached its peak when their six single-seaters were reinforced by a similar number of radar-equipped Me 262B two-seater nightfighters (converted on the Messerschmitt assembly lines from partially completed trainers).

It was intended that the Me 262Bs should infiltrate the bomber stream during the raiders' approach and then utilise their own airborne search radar to locate and destroy individual targets. But the jet's excess of speed, which played such an essential part in the single-seaters' success in catching searchlight-illuminated Mosquitos (Welter's January trio of kills had already assured him of 'ace status' on the Me 262), proved a distinct disadvantage against the RAF's four-engined 'heavies'. Despite the antler-like, nose-mounted, antenna of the SN-2 Lichtenstein radar, which helped to make the Me 262B some 60 kmh slower than its single-seat counterpart, it was still all too easy to overshoot a lumbering, fully-loaded, bomber. The 'Berta' crews quickly evolved their own tactics to combat this, however. They would fly along *below* the bomber stream and endeavour to lose sufficient speed in the last few seconds' climb to their chosen victim.

But it was the Mosquito which continued to provide the most frequent targets for Welter's single-seater pilots. They dubbed the almost nightly raids on their capital the 'Berlin Express', and became so familiar with the RAF's three favoured routes of approach that they christened them simply 'platforms 1, 2 and 3'!

During the final ten days of March 1945, Feldwebel Karl-Heinz Becker, who had already

claimed a P-38 by day in mid-February, enjoyed a remarkable run of success when he shot down six Mosquitos. His combat report of 31 March describes the last of these encounters;

'Took off at 2129 hrs (30 March) for night patrol Berlin area. Immediate contact with enemy aircraft (E/A). Attacked from astern at altitude of 8000 m. E/A evaded my fire by climbing and breaking to port . . . I circled and attacked a second time; target now above me and to the right. I opened fire while still in the turn, leading the target which flew through this salvo. I observed multiple hits on the fuselage and starboard wing. The enemy aircraft rolled to port and went down inverted, followed by our searchlights. It went into a steep dive before hitting the ground. From an altitude of 8500 m I observed the crash at 2152 hrs in grid FG 5/5.'

That same night Kurt Welter, who had received the Oak Leaves to his Knight's Cross less than a fortnight earlier, underlined his mastery by claiming no fewer than four Mosquitos (although so far only one of his alleged victims on this date has been tentatively identified – and this may even have been Becker's kill detailed above).

Despite being unarmed, it was a Mosquito which, albeit unwittingly, was indirectly responsible for what is believed to be the unit's only two-seater operational loss. Leutnant Herbert Altner was an experienced nightfighter with NJG 5 (he had already scored 21 kills) when, sometime in February 1945, Kurt Welter chanced to land at his Lübeck base. Altner's expressed interest in the twin-engined jet led to his joining the Welter fold at Burg the following month.

After the usual familiarisation process – two circuits of the field by day, two by night – Altner had become the first pilot to fly the two-seater Me 262B operationally. But his 'conversion' had perhaps been a shade *too* perfunctory, for one night later in March, 'We were vectored towards a group of Mosquitos. When we gained contact with one of

An early Me 262A-2a bomber of 1./KG 51 ('9K+YH'), pictured at Achmer, displays an unusual 'scribble' camouflage scheme and the *Geschwader*'s penchant for *Staffel* colour coding – i.e. white individual aircraft letter, nosecap and vertical tailfin tip. As the war entered its closing weeks, many KG 51 machines found their way into Galland's JV 44

As mentioned earlier, Allied fighter pilots quickly discovered that the Me 262 was at its most vulnerable when taking off or on approach to landing. The RAF employed the term 'Rat Catching' to describe the process of attacking the Me 262 shortly before the jet entered the protective field of fire given by the 'Flak Lanes', established some five to eight miles outside the airfield perimeter. Attacking Me 262s in this way was a dangerous practice, for the 'Flak Lanes' accounted for many Allied fighters, although successes did occur. This touched-up USAAF P-47 gun camera photo records the finals moments of a Me 262, under-carriage lowered and about to receive the *coup-de-grace* (*via Aeroplane Monthly*)

This rare shot shows JV 44 Me 262A-1a 'White 5', which was the mount of Unteroffizier Eduard Schallmoser during the final weeks of war (*via Robert Forsyth*)

the fast Engländer, I pushed the throttle wide open. Much more quickly than I had expected, the "Mossie" loomed large in my gun-sight. Somewhat taken aback, I eased off the throttle a touch too abruptly'. A certain recipe for a flame-out, and sure enough, 'My two "ovens" didn't take at all kindly to this treatment, and both promptly went out. The "Me" began to lose speed, but I couldn't restart them. With the aircraft in imminent danger of crashing, there was no choice but to bale out. Unfortunately my radar-operator, Feldwebel Reinhard Lommatzsch, must have struck the tail in so doing, for he was discovered dead on the ground'.

By now the end was rapidly approaching. As with most other units, it was hastened by a lack of fuel and the proximity of the enemy, both on the ground and in the air above. On 10 April a daylight raid on Burg resulted in the destruction of three of the *Kommando*'s aircraft.

Forty-eight hours later, with Soviet troops approaching Berlin from the east, the four surviving machines decamped northwards to Lübeck. They had been here for little more than a week before another Allied air raid caused further casualties, among them one of the few remaining two-seaters, which was reportedly buried beneath a collapsing hangar roof.

From the debris of Lübeck-Blankensee airfield it was but a ten-kilometre hop to the Autobahn leading southwards out of the city in the direction of Hamburg. Hiding their jets under the trees lining the Autobahn, they used a straight, stretch of carriageway near the Reinfeld exit as a makeshift runway, for amazingly, pilots were still being despatched to Rechlin to ferry back replacement machines.

But in reality the *Kommando* was on its last legs and almost inactive. It is recorded that Kurt Welter, by now the highest-scoring Me 262 ace of them all, had not flown on operations since the unit's departure from Burg. One final move took it to Schleswig-Jagel on 7 May, where it was to await the arrival of the occupying British forces. The aircraft of *Kommando Welter* (aka 10./NJG 11) – four single-seaters and a pair of radar-equipped two-seaters – were lined up alongside the Schleswig runway as ordered. Several of the pilots, however, elected to end their time with the unit even more informally than when they had first been invited by Welter to join it. Herbert Altner, for one, quite simply got on his bike and pedalled home!

Three days before *Kommando Welter* flew in to Schleswig, in the far north of Germany, to hand its aircraft over to the British, another unit – at the southern extremity of the now divided Reich – had placed hand grenades in the engine nacelles of its Me 262s to deny them to the approaching American army.

This act marked the demise of a formation which was unique within the ranks of the wartime Luftwaffe, and which was to become the subject of continued controversy in Germany for decades afterwards – its supporters calling it the 'Squadron of Experts', its detractors likening it to a select club whose importance was inflated by a band of postwar self-publicists.

It had all begun in the deteriorating relationship between the frontline fighter commanders and the Luftwaffe's upper hierarchy, represented by Hermann Göring and a small coterie of his closest advisers. Things came to a head at the end of 1944 when the Reichsmarschall, persuaded that the 'poor' performance of the *Jagdwaffe* was the cause of all his ills, dismissed his *General der Jagdflieger*, Adolf Galland. Although couched in conciliatory and diplomatic terms (an 'Order of the Day to the Fighter Arm', dated 23 January 1945, would begin: 'After several years in office Generalleutnant Galland has been relieved of his post as the *General der Jagdflieger* in order that he may resume a

Me 262A-1a Wk-Nr 110559 'Red 13' was the mount of Oberstleutnant Heinz Bär, *Kommandeur* of III./EJG 2 at Lechfeld in March 1945. He became the leading daylight jet ace in the final months of the war, with only Kurt Welter bettering Bär's score of 16 victories. Prior to flying the Me 262, Bär was already one of the Luftwaffe's highest scoring pilots, with over 200 kills to his credit. Not only was he a highly proficient ace, but he was also a fine fighter leader. Although Bär first flew the Me 262 in September 1944, it was not until January 1945 that he was posted to Lager-Lechfeld to command III./EJG 2. Whilst this unit was primarily a training *Gruppe*, Bär nevertheless managed to achieve nine victories during his time there, before being transferred to substitute for Galland, who retained effective non-flying control, at JV44 during April 1945. Once here, he continued to score freely, gaining his 16th, and final, jet victory on 28 April 1945. Bär was killed 12 years later in 1957 when his light aircraft crashed near Brunswick

Oberstleutnant Heinz Bär is seen sitting on the wing of 'Red 13' discussing the maintenance of his jet with one of his 'blackmen' between sorties at Lechfeld in early 1945

III./EJG 2 pilot Leutnant Karl 'Fox' Munz arrived late onto jet operations from 3./JG 52, seeing combat during the last six weeks of the war with the conversion unit. Not to be denied, he managed to score three kills with the Me 262 to add to his 60 attained with conventional fighters. Munz had completed over 600 sorties duirng his five years of uninterrupted combat flying

position of leadership when his health has recovered'), this proved to be the last straw.

On 19 January a delegation of high-ranking combat *Kommodoren* had confronted Göring at a meeting convened at the 'Haus der Flieger', the Luftwaffe officers' club, in Berlin. Their elected spokesman, Oberst Günther Lützow, a *Condor Legion* ace and *Kommodore* of JG 3 during the Battle of Britain (see *Aircraft of the Aces 11 - Bf 109D/E Aces 1939-41*), outlined their grievances. These included the charges of cowardice brought against them, the mismanagement of available forces, and the growing influence of 'outsiders' in purely fighter affairs (this latter a clear reference to the 'bomber barons' now surrounding Göring, one of whom – Generalmajor Dietrich Peltz – had been the brains behind the catastrophic and costly Operation *Bodenplatte*, the *Jagdwaffe's* New Year's Day attack on Allied fighter airfields less than three weeks earlier).

In talks lasting nearly five hours, a demand was also made for Galland's reinstatement. But the underlying theme was a condemnation of the Reichsmarschall's own inflexibly autocratic control of the

Me 262A-1a Wk-Nr 170056 was a true workhorse within the Messerschmitt test programme, being used for both directional stability trials and nighfighter aerodynamic work. Seen here in late 1944 carrying out the latter series of trials, the Me 262 has its cannon compartment doors hinged open, allowing factory armourers access to the jet's quartet of MK 108 cannon

Luftwaffe at a time when changes were desperately needed to stave off defeat. At the close of proceedings an apoplectic Göring's immediate reaction was to threaten to have Lützow shot. In fact, arrest warrants were issued within hours for both Lützow *and* Galland (although not present at the 'Haus der Flieger' meeting, the latter was branded a fellow 'mutineer'). But upon reflection, Lützow's punishment was reduced to exile. He was banished to Verona, in Italy, as Jafü Oberitalien (Fighter-leader Upper Italy).

Galland's fate, endorsed by his successor as *General der Jagdflieger*, Oberst Gordon Gollob, was to have been a posting to the Russian front as *Staffelkapitän* of 4./JG 54. Compared to such a demotion

Rare shot of a flightline of Me 262B-1a/U1s belonging to 10./NJG 11 *Kommando Welter*, based at Burg, near Magdeburg, some 70 miles west of Berlin (*via Manfred Jurleit*)

(assigning a Generalleutnant to the command of a *Staffel*), even the lowest point of Heinz Bär's legendary rollercoaster career would have paled into insignificance! But salvation came from an unexpected quarter. Adolf Hitler had known nothing of the incipient revolt. When he learned of it, he ordered instead that Galland be instructed to set up a small, *Staffel*-strength, unit to demonstrate the Me 262's superiority as a fighter.

The Führer's decree was something of a face-saving redundancy. The Me 262's potential had already been amply 'demonstrated' by EKdo 262 and the *Kommando Nowotny*. And although this new command of Galland's was also initially intended to be of only *Staffel* strength, it was granted complete independence, while he himself was given the disciplinary powers of a divisional commander.

He chose as his base Brandenburg-Briest, some 45 kilometres to the west of Berlin. Here he would be ideally placed to assist in the defence of the capital. On a more practical level, this airfield also housed elements of JG 7, from whom Galland hoped to obtain some material assistance. In this he was to be disappointed. Gordon Gollob stuck rigidly to the letter that the new formation "was not to influence other units in any way whatsoever". Galland was later to complain that the incumbent *General der Jagdflieger* thwarted his every move, particularly his requests for key personnel. Gollob refuted this charge vehemently, pointing out (not unreasonably) that frontline fighter units were already chronically short of experienced leaders, and that Galland could not be allowed to cream off the best of those that remained 'for his own personal use to the detriment of the fighting fronts'.

Consequently, he was only allowed to have those of his own ilk, 'disgraced' by association with the 'Haus der Flieger' meeting (most notably Johannes 'Mäcki' Steinhoff, latterly *Kommodore* of JG 7, who was appointed 'Head of Training'), and those who were convalescing or recovering from wounds, together with a leavening of instructors and newly-qualified trainees. Gradually, however, word spread and others were to join via more 'unofficial' channels – not only acknowledged fighter *Experten*, but pilots from nightfighter, bomber and

Major Wilhelm 'Willi' Herget – the ex-nightfighter ace shown here wearing the Oak Leaves won during his time as *Gruppenkommandeur* of I./NJG 4 – arrived at JV 44 in the experimental 50 mm cannon-armed Me 262A-1a/U4 (see opposite and profile number 23), which he had been testing at Lechfeld

Me 262B-1a/U1 'interim' nightfighter (ex-10./NJG 11) after surrender to the British at Schleswig and transfer to the Americans, whose 'Foreign Equipment' number (FE-610) may be seen in white below the tailplane. Here, it is shown on display at Melun, in France, on 27 June 1945, awaiting inspection by Gen Carl Spaatz, prior to shipment to the US

Close-up of the experimental 50 mm Mauser MK 214 cannon installed in the nose of Wk-Nr 111899, the aircraft subsequently flown to Munich-Riem by Willi Herget when he joined JV 44

ground-attack units as well. And this despite one final pettiness – the ex-*General der Jagdflieger* was not to use his own name to promulgate his new unit. In other words, there was to be no '*Kommando Galland*'. Instead, he chose the title *Jagdverband* 44, 'Jagdverband' meaning simply fighter unit, the '44' supposedly being an oblique and convoluted reference to a number of issues, including the year of the *Jagdwaffe*'s decline, half the value of his very first command (3.J/88, a fighter *Staffel* of the *Condor Legion* in Spain) and a derogatory word play on the title of his one-time benefactor, and recent saviour, Adolf Hitler.

The whole of March 1945 was spent in training and working up the embryonic JV 44. Only one operational sortie is known of during this period – that described by Steinhoff himself when he led a *Kette* of three Me 262s eastwards across Berlin towards the Russian front along the River Oder. Near Strausberg they spotted a group of Soviet Il-2 *Sturmovik* ground-attack aircraft strafing a German convoy. Despite their difference in speed, Steinhoff managed to line up one of the attackers in his sights. A split-second burst from his four nose cannon was enough to send the heavily-armoured 'Ivan' bellying into the snow

This three-quarter frontal view of one of the two Me 262A1a/U4 prototypes completed before the end of the war clearly illustrates the modified nosewheel which swivelled through 90° during retraction to lie flat beneath the cannon, whose bulk occupied most of the forward fuselage

alongside the road. This was probably the very first of JV 44's estimated 56 kills, and also one of only a handful of Soviet aircraft to fall victim to the Me 262.

By the end of March Galland had come to the conclusion that the protection of the Messerschmitt jet production plants in southern Germany was more vital to the continuation of the war effort than the aerial defence of the sprawling metropolis of Berlin. On the last day of the month his Me 262s began transferring down to Munich-Riem. They were followed by a parting shot from Oberst Gollob who, in a four-page report on jet fighter operations dated 3 April 1945 and circulated among all Luftwaffe higher staffs up to and including the Reichsmarschall himself, had this to say of their performance in the Berlin area to date;

'So far *Jagdverband* 44 has achieved nothing, even though it contains a number of very good pilots. Furthermore, it is pursuing operational methods which are not merely at variance with, but actually counter-productive to, commonly accepted principles. It is proposed that the unit be disbanded and its pilots be employed more usefully within the ranks of other existing units.'

Me 262 V303 Wk-Nr 170303 is seen being loaded with SC 500-kg bombs during the '*Schnellstbomber*' test programme. As a result of these trials, *Kommando Stamp* was formed on 27 December 1944 (led by Major Gerhard Stamp) with the intention of attacking heavy bomber formations withAB 500-kg and SC 250-kg bombs. *Kommando Stamp* was equipped with Me 262A-2as, and duly reported some success with the larger AB 500-kg weapons

Hauptmann Walter Krupinski was another legendary Luftwaffe ace who ended his career flying Me 262s with JV 44 during the final weeks of the war. He notched-up two jet kills to add to his piston-engined tally of 195 victories

But Galland continued to go his own way. A safe distance from the internal squabbles of Berlin, he began to recruit more pilots, to accept delivery of more new aircraft from the nearby Messerschmitt factories, and to equip them with the latest R4M air-to-air rockets already being used to such devastating effect by JG 7.

On 4 April JV 44 scored its opening success against the Americans when Unteroffizier Eduard Schallmoser, one of the original trainee intake, misjudged his closing speed and clipped the tail of a P-38 Lightning near Munich. It was the first of several such incidents which would earn Schallmoser the nickname of the 'Jet rammer'. Twenty-four hours later the unit claimed its first 'heavy', a B-17 shot down by a formation of five Me 262s led by 'Mäcki' Steinhoff.

The move from Brandenburg down to Munich did, however, have one severe disadvantage. It took them straight into the 'eye of the storm' of the US air offensive against Germany's jet production centres and fighter airfields. JV 44 suffered severe material losses in the middle two weeks of April. A concentrated B-17 raid on the Munich area in the late afternoon of 9 April cratered the main runway at Riem and damaged six Me 262s. The following day ground-strafing P-51s accounted for three more jets damaged, plus three destroyed. And so it went on, with a growing number of Me 262s being lost on the ground to enemy fighter-bombers patrolling overhead 'for what seemed like hours at a time' and ready to pounce on the slightest movement. Galland did try to organise his own airfield protection unit of Focke-Wulf Fw 190D-9s, but they failed to bring down a single attacker.

Despite the constant attrition, JV 44's numbers were sustained by a steady influx of new aircraft. More pilots kept arriving from all quar-

This Me 262, minus its two Jumo 004 powerplants, was captured on film by an RAF scientific team visiting Germany at the end of the war. The RAF released the photo on 29 November 1945, and it clearly shows that this Me 262 had been hidden from Allied attack in trees alongside the Autobahn

At the end of the war Me 262s (both production models and important experimental types) were reduced to broken hulks. For such an innovative marque it was a sad end. The Germans themselves sought to immobilise the aircraft by strapping an explosive charge to the nose gear oleo, thus preventing the Allies from making use of the jet. Many Me 262s were also booby trapped with 5-lb blocks of TNT underneath the pilot's seat. In the event, very few survived into the postwar years, and of those that did, only eight genuine examples are in existence today – none of which has flown since the late 1940s. This shot shows Me 262s in various states of disrepair outside the former experimental hangar at Lager-Lechfeld. Amongst the wreckage can be seen one of the most significant Me 262s ever built – namely Me 262 V9 'VI+AD' Wk-Nr 130004 (to the left of the photo), which was used primarily as a high speed test bed, equipped with, amongst other modifications, a streamlined racing cockpit

ters too. Among the newcomers at this juncture were three highly-decorated *Experten*. Firstly, Oberst Günther Lützow, the 'arch-conspirator' himself, back from Italy after personally pleading his case with the Reichsmarschall, and now granted permission to join JV 44. The second-highest scoring fighter pilot in history, 301-victory Russian front veteran Major Gerhard Barkhorn, arrived via more unofficial channels while recuperating from wounds received earlier.

The world's highest scorer and one of Barkhorn's fellow *Gruppenkommandeure* in JG 52, the legendary Erich Hartmann, had previously declined an invitation from Galland to throw in his lot with JV 44, preferring to remain with his colleagues in the east.

And from the nightfighter arm, via the Lechfeld test centre, came Major Wilhelm Herget, whose 57 nocturnal victories – gained after an initial 14 as a *Zerstörer* pilot – included eight claimed in the space of just fifty minutes on the night of 20 December 1943. Herget reportedly arrived at Munich-Riem in the aircraft he had been testing at Lechfeld. This was fitted with a gigantic 50 mm Mauser cannon projecting from its nose. The diminutive Willi Herget, known to all in the Luftwaffe as 'der Kleine' ('Titch'), certainly flew this Me 262 on subsequent operations – one American flyer who witnessed it in the air likened it to having a 'giant telegraph pole' sticking out the front – but fortunately for Herget's intended victims this monstrosity was very prone to jamming.

Galland used the far more effective R4M rockets to bring down a pair of B-26 Marauders on 16 April (see *Combat Aircraft 2 - B-26 Units of the Eighth and Nonth Air Forces*), but forty-eight hours later, as he was taking off with five other aircraft against yet more incoming bombers, JV 44 suffered its first serious casualty. Galland and his two wingmen lifted off cleanly. In their wake the leader of the second *Kette*, Major Steinhoff, gathered speed across Riem's uneven grassy surface. The repair gangs had not made a very good job of filling in the previous days' craters, and at nearly 200 kmh Steinhoff suffered catastrophic gear failure – probably from a burst tyre. The port undercarriage leg collapsed, the left wing dropped and the uncontrollable Me 262 hit the perimeter embankment and exploded. Somehow, Steinhoff managed to escape from the inferno of blazing fuel and detonating rockets, but he would be disfigured for the rest of his life.

But operations continued. On 19 April JV 44 claimed one B-26 destroyed and one probable, followed 24 hours later by a further seven Marauders damaged and three shot down three – two of the latter fell victim to R4Ms launched by Unteroffizier Johann-Karl Müller, a veteran Fw 190 ground-attack pilot. One of the damaged B-26s, incidentally, had been clipped by Eduard Schallmoser (the 'Jet rammer'), who then had to bale out himself . . . only to land in the garden of his own parental home outside Munich!

23 April saw a sudden increase in both aircraft and pilots as Major Heinz Bär and his III./EJG 2 arrived from Lechfeld, and I./KG 51's Me 262s flew in from Memmingen. Both *Gruppen* put themselves at JV 44's disposal. This meant that Galland's nominal '*Staffel*' now comprised over 40 available machines (and more than double that figure if the Me 262s undergoing conversion and repair at Riem were taken into account) and 90+ pilots, although some 50 of these were still classified as trainees.

Numbers alone do not make a unit, however. It was the 'inner circle' of high-scoring *Experten* around Galland which gave JV 44 its individuality. It was they who wore the decorations which prompted much of the later cynicism – 'A unit emblem wasn't necessary. They treated the Knight's Cross as a sort of club badge', was one such comment that the *Jagdverband's* core of aces provoked from an outsider. But it was also the so called 'inner circle' which felt most the loss of one of their own.

After nearly three years' absence from combat flying, Günther Lützow was finding the Me 262 difficult to master. He nevertheless managed to claim a B-26 on the morning of 24 April. That same afternoon he betrayed his inexperience. Bounced by P-47s while attacking another formation of Marauders, Lützow dived to escape. He started to pull out, but then – presumably realising that two P-47s were still on his tail – suddenly entered an even steeper dive from which he never recovered. His machine went straight into the ground and exploded.

The next 72 hours saw JV 44's final sorties from Munich-Riem. On 25 April – the day the Reich was split in two by the Americans and the Soviets' linking up on the Elbe – Unteroffizier Franz Köster downed a

The retrieval of Me 262s for evaluation by the RAF and USAAF in May/June 1945 has entered into military aviation folklore. This low flying display in a Me 262 was performed by either Lt Robert C Strobell or Col Harold Watson, the latter individual being the commanding officer of the USAAF's Air Technical Intelligence team, which was subsequently christened 'Watson's Whizzers'. This flight took place in front Gen Spaatz at Melun on 27 June 1945. The general was clearly most impressed with what he saw, for afterwards he came over to Watson and said 'Hal, that's a wicked aeroplane. Wicked. WICKED! I'm sure glad that they (the Luftwaffe) screwed up the tactical use of this aeroplane'. Watson replied 'They really did, sir'

P-51 and a P-38 to add to the three earlier kills he had achieved when with JG 7. The following day JV 44 scrambled a dozen R4M-equipped Me 262s, led by Galland himself, to intercept a mixed Franco-American force of B-26 Marauders attacking targets north of Munich.

In the engagement which followed four of the B-26s were brought down. Two fell to the cannon of Adolf Galland, who, distracted by accurate return fire from the tail gunners of the closely-formated bombers, had tripped only one of the two safety switches necessary to release his rockets. A third Marauder was claimed by his wingman, Unteroffizier Schallmoser, who on this occasion *did* use his rockets rather than his customary, if involuntary, ramming tactics!

Galland's machine had, in fact, suffered damage during his attack on the bombers. He was then caught again by one of the P-47 fighter escorts which 'split-essed' down on him unseen. A two-second burst from the Thunderbolt's eight 0.50s scored hits in the Me 262's starboard wing root area before Galland managed to break left and disappear into the clouds. With his right engine cowling flapping loose in the wind, his instrument panel shattered and shrapnel embedded in his right knee, Galland nursed the jet back to Riem, where he made a deadstick landing – trailing smoke and with a punctured nose wheel – in the middle of a low-level fighter-bomber raid!

The Generalleutnant leaped from his crippled machine and quickly sought cover. The operational career of arguably the most distinguished wartime Luftwaffe fighter leader of them all had thus come full circle – begun six years earlier as a ground-attack pilot in Poland, it ended in the welcome haven of a nearby bomb crater with Galland himself now the target of ground-strafing enemy aircraft.

Heinz Bär immediately assumed operational control of JV 44. Like Willi Herget, Bär had also arrived at JV 44 bringing a specially armed

This highly distinctive Me 262A-1a/U4 (Wk-Nr 170083) was initially christened *Wilma Jeanne* by MSgt Eugene E Freiburger of the 54th Air Disarmament Squadron (ADS) following its acquisition by the USAAF – it was subsequently renamed *Happy Hunter II* by Col Watson. Seen at Lager-Lechfeld, this jet was reduced to a smouldering pile of wreckage when, on the flight across France to Cherbourg, it suffered engine failure and its pilot, former Messerschmitt test pilot Ludwig Hoffmann, was forced to parachute to safety. The latter individual was slightly injured during the incident, and to make matters worse, he had to endure a hostile interrogation by French farm-hands upon landing

Me 262 with him. In his case, it was a machine fitted with an additional brace of nose cannon. On the day after Galland's wounding, Bär, flying this six-gunned aircraft and with Willi Herget and Franz Köster as his wingmen, broke up a group of American fighters busily engaged yet again in attacking Munich-Riem. Bär and Köster claimed two P-47s apiece, with Herget downing one (the latter was presumably flying a standard Me 262 at the time, not the machine equipped with the recalcitrant 50 mm 'telegraph pole', which was specifically an anti-bomber weapon, and hardly suited to dog-fighting).

Overcrowded, suffering almost continual air attacks, and directly in the path of the rapidly approaching US Seventh Army, Munich-Riem was clearly no longer inhabitable. On 28 April JV 44 was therefore ordered to Hörsching, in Austria. But, exercising his independence to the last, Galland decided his unit would be better served if it transferred to Salzburg-Maxglan instead. This they did on the same day, only to be greeted by that airfield's trigger-happy flak defences – fortunately without loss.

By now it was all academic anyway, as was JV 44's last-minute conversion (on paper, at least) into IV./JG 7. Only one operational sortie was mounted out of Maxglan, with Heinz Bär's six-cannon Me 262 destroying one last P-47 over Bad Aibling on 29 April. Within the week General Patch's tenacious Seventh Army had caught up with them again – the town of Salzburg surrendered on 4 May 1945. And with Sherman tanks of the 20th Armoured Division probing out towards Maxglan airfield, it fell to 197-victory *Experte*, and Russian front veteran, Major Walter Krupinski to close the chapter on JV 44 by placing hand grenades in the engine nacelles of each of the unit's two-dozen or so remaining aircraft.

Cannibalisation of Me 262s took place in the partially damaged hangar which the 54th ADS used as their workshop. They USAAF groundcrews soon discovered that nose sections were interchangeable, as this photograph clearly illustrates

OTHER UNITS, OTHER TYPES

In addition to the units described in the previous chapters, a number of other formations flew the Me 262 fighter. Among these were the *Industrieschutzstaffeln* (literally Industry Protection Squadrons) which, as their title suggests, were small units set up by the aircraft manufacturers themselves to defend their own plants and facilities. Most of these factory defence squadrons took the name of their parent company, and were manned by the works' test pilots. The two such Me 262 units, however, (each consisting of six aircraft) appear to have been formed on a more official level.

They were identified numerically (ISS 1 and 2, which were intended for the defence of the assembly plants at Leipheim and Schwäbisch Hall respectively), their personnel were drawn for the most part from the Luftwaffe, and they were subordinated to the *7.Jagddivision*. Activated early in January 1945 for an intended trial period of two months, both were incorporated into larger existing formations (JG 7 and JV 44) at the beginning of February.

There were several other 'named' formations, ranging in size from the likes of the *Gefechtsverband* (Combat unit) *Hogeback*, which was made up of the remains of the various *Gruppen* that found themselves concentrated at Prague's Ruzyn airport in the closing days of the war, right down to such as the experimental *Kommando Gladenbeck*, which numbered just one Me 262 among the five aircraft it operated out of Parchin late in January 1945.

It is not known whether either of the ISSs, or any of the miscellany of named *Kommandos*, scored any victories – certainly they produced no aces. But there *was* one other unit which was credited with something like 50 kills.

The original policy which had decreed that the Me 262 be deployed solely as a bomber, and which had so prejudiced its early career, underwent a complete reversal. Within six months plans were being drawn up to convert many long-established bomber units on to the Me 262 to reinforce the fighter arm. Apart from KG 51, which was to remain officially a bomber formation throughout (although here too some elements were later incorporated into JV 44), almost a third of existing bomber strength was scheduled to re-equip. The course of events prevented this programme from being carried out, and only one such bomber unit, KG 54, saw action in any numbers.

Although redesignated KG(J) 54 on 1 October 1944 (the 'J' denoting its quasi-fighter role), retraining progressed very slowly. Its first real operational deployment did not begin until mid-December when it mounted sporadic fighter-bomber attacks on American ground

Oberstleutnant Volprecht Riedesel Freiherr von Eisenbach, *Kommodore* of KG(J) 54. Shown here wearing the Knight's Cross awarded on 7 October 1942 while serving as *Kommandeur* of II./KG 76, Baron von Riedesel commanded KG 54 for more than two years – and had won the Oak Leaves – before being killed in action on 9 February 1945 (see profile number 26)

forces during the Battle of the Ardennes. And it was February 1945 before the first effective missions against the US daylight bombing offensive were flown. On 9 February, for example, I./KG 54 accounted for two of the five B-17s lost, but only at a cost of four of their own number (including the *Geschwaderkommodore*, who had elected to lead the *Gruppe* that day).

In the closing three months of the war they reportedly claimed some 50 Allied aircraft destroyed. But they too paid a high price. Not only in action, but also as a result of accidents and in the continuous bombing and strafing of their home bases. By the war's end, which saw them reverting to fighter-bomber missions in the areas south of Berlin, they had lost over 70 per cent of their total inventory of 150+ Me 262s.

Once again, it is unlikely that they produced any aces, but one of their best candidates for the accolade was perhaps 3.*Staffel*'s Leutnant Bernhard Becker (not to be confused with the nightfighting Karl-Heinz Becker), who claimed two B-17s on 10 April 1945 to add to the one he had shot down north of Hannover six days earlier.

And while on the subject of 'non-aces', brief mention should also be made – if only for the sake of completeness – of the three other jet types flown operationally by the Luftwaffe.

The Arado company, whose Ar 234 twin-jet bomber had been instrumental in releasing the Me 262 for fighter production, were anxious that their design too should be considered for other roles. In fact, it made a superb reconnaissance machine, able to overfly the United Kingdom with impunity. But as a nightfighter it was less successful.

The highly experienced nightfighter pilot Kurt Welter, whose expert opinion was sought by the OKL, had been asked to fly comparison tests of both the Me 262 and the Ar 234. He came down strongly in favour of the former. Among his main criticisms of the Arado was the extensive glazing of the pilot's position in the extreme nose. Not only did this distort peripheral vision, and thus make night take-offs and

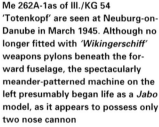

Me 262A-1as of III./KG 54 'Totenkopf' are seen at Neuburg-on-Danube in March 1945. Although no longer fitted with *'Wikingerschiff'* weapons pylons beneath the forward fuselage, the spectacularly meander-patterned machine on the left presumably began life as a *Jabo* model, as it appears to possess only two nose cannon

landings all the more hazardous, it offered virtually no protection against flying debris from a target being attacked from astern. It also meant that nose armament was an impracticality and would necessitate the bolting on of external gun packs.

Despite these observations, a small experimental nightfighter unit, the *Kommando Bisping*, was established. But when Hauptmann Josef Bisping, a Knight's Cross reconnaissance pilot, was killed in a take-off accident on 23 February 1945, command passed to Hauptmann Kurt Bonow, whose previous service with NJGs 5 and 100 had netted him some ten nocturnal kills. Flying the Ar 234 as leader (and sole operational pilot) of the *Kommando Bonow* during the final ten weeks of the war, he managed on several occasions to intercept RAF Mosquito night intruders but failed to add to his score.

As it transpired, the only type apart from the Me 262 to achieve any confirmed victories was that other product of the Messerschmitt stable, the Me 163. In comparison, however, the Me 163's success was negligible. Nor was it a true jet aircraft, instead being rocket-powered. And it was this rocket, together with its associated fuel system, which was the Me 163's undoing. If Messerschmitt had suffered problems with the Junkers Jumo turbojet powerplants of the Me 262, their experience with the Walter rocket engine of the Me 163 was a nightmare.

Such was the volatile nature of the mix of the two different fuels required to power the rocket that the slightest leak, or anything but the smoothest of take-offs or landing runs, could result in a violent explosion. Pilots would later be advised that, in the event of an emergency landing, they should clamber out on to the wing as soon as possible, roll themselves into a ball, and take their chances hitting the ground at anything up to 150 km/h rather than ride the skidding Me 163 to almost inevitable destruction. If the rocket failed on take-off there was hardly any chance at all. Instant death was usually the result. And these were the lucky ones. For the rocket fuels were also highly corrosive. Any pilot unfortunate enough to suffer an accident which did not

Although discovered by US troops in a wrecked hangar at Manching in Bavaria surrounded by Ju 88G nightfighters, this Arado Ar 234 is not a *Kommando Bonow* machine. But the sorry state of the cockpit certainly bears out Kurt Welter's assertion that the type was not suited for nightfighting

Me 163B-1a Wk-Nr 191301 wears a prominent US Foreign Equipment serial on its tail. This particular fighter was test-glided over Edwards Air Force Base (AFB), California, in 1946, before being stored by the USAF at Norton AFB, again in California. Presented to the National Air and Space Museum in 1954, the Me 163 is now on display at the museum's reserve facility at Silver Hill, in Maryland

immediately blow himself and his aircraft to pieces, but who found himself trapped in wreckage surrounded by leaking fuel, was quite literally dissolved alive!

Operationally, too, the rocket was a disaster. Its manufacturers, the Walter company of Kiel-Tannenberg, had initially promised a running time of 12 minutes. But after extensive and prolonged tests, this was reduced to barely four minutes. This in turn made a nonsense of the planned deployment of the Me 163, which had envisaged a chain of bases, some 150 km apart, stretching across the major approach routes of the enemy bomber streams. Four minutes fuel would allow just time enough for take-off and a near vertical climb to the bombers' normal operating altitude, with very little to spare for combat manoeuvring.

And when an alternative scheme for mobile Me 163 units to be mounted on special railway trains came to naught, the rocket fighter was effectively reduced to a point interceptor, able only to defend a specific objective within its immediate vicinity. And no amount of

An award-winning prewar glider pilot, Major Wolfgang Späte went on to become a highly successful fighter ace, before joining the Me 163 development programme as a test pilot. After enjoying no success with the rocket fighter, Späte eventually led the Me 262-equipped III./JG 7 during the latter part of the war, scoring exactly five kills. He had first flown the Me 262 back in April 1943

rhetoric – 'If the Me 262 was the broadsword, cutting swathes through the oncoming bombers, then the Me 163 was the rapier, lancing cleanly upwards to dispatch the enemy over the target' — could disguise the fact.

The first Me 163 service test unit, *Erprobungskommando* 16, had been set up in May 1942 under Oberleutnant Wolfgang Späte, a 72-victory *Experte* who had been recalled from the Russian front only days earlier to be awarded the Oak Leaves to his Knight's Cross. Späte was also a well-

known pre-war glider pilot, as were several other members of EKdo 16, the Me 163 design having started life as an unpowered glider.)

Two long years of frustration followed. It was not until 14 May 1944 that Späte, by now a Major, attempted the first operational mission in the rocket fighter. Vectored on to a pair of P-47s flying near the Bad Zwischnenahn test field, Späte was just closing in to attack when his rocket motor cut out. Fortunately (or should it be astoundingly), neither enemy pilot had spotted the tomato-red Me 163 (specially painted for the occasion by Späte's ground-crew!), and he returned safely to base after restarting the motor.

By this time, however, the first operational *Staffel* had been formed from the ranks of EKdo 16 and had departed for Wittmundhafen as 20./JG 1, under the command of Hauptmann Robert Olejnik. It was from here – the *Staffel*, in the meantime, having already been redesignated 1.//JG 400 – that the first combat mission was flown, also unsuccessfully, when Unteroffizier Konrad Schiebeler ran out of fuel while climbing to intercept a reconnaissance Lightning on 7 July.

In the following weeks the unit, now risen to *Gruppe* strength, was transferred to Brandis, east of Leipzig. Henceforth, their role was to be the defence of the oil refinery complex at Leuna-Merseburg, some 40 km away on the far side of the city *(Gruppenkommandeur* Hauptmann Rudolf Opitz's complaints that there were more suitable airfields nearer to Leuna had fallen on deaf ears).

The US daylight air offensive against Germany's oil industry was at its height, and several intercepts had been made on B-17 formations, without tangible results, before July was out. It was in early August 1944 (the exact date is unfortunately unknown) when Leutnant

A ground mechanic uses a funnel to gingerly top up the 'C' Stoff tank of Me 163B 'White 06' in preparation for take-off . . .

Hartmut Ryll claimed the Me 163's first combat kill, a B-17 downed during a midday sortie. About a fortnight later Feldwebel Siegfried Schubert got the second by blowing the entire tail unit off another B-17 with just three rounds from his 30 mm MK 108 cannon. But it was during this same engagement, on 16 August, that the *Gruppe* lost Hartmut Ryll, who fell victim to two of the bombers' P-51D fighter escort.

On 24 August Feldwebel Schubert destroyed two more 'heavies', with Leutnant Hans Bott and Feldwebel Strassnicky later downing one apiece. Unteroffizier Schiebeler, whose shortage of fuel had denied him the Lightning on 7 July, more than made up for it by bringing down a four-engined bomber in full view of everybody at Brandis on 11 September, and then claiming another over Merseburg just twenty-four hours later. These were the *Gruppe*'s seventh and eight victories. They would not get very many more, despite an increase in strength over the coming weeks, with a *Geschwaderstab* JG 400 being formed under Major Wolfgang Späte, and a II. *Gruppe* being established to the north at Stargard to defend the nearby Pölitz hydroelectric plant.

In fact, the remainder of 1944 was a period of almost unrelieved gloom with few, if any, successes and mounting losses, both in combat and in a succession of accidents. On 7 October, for example, I./JG 400 put up some 20 Me 163s against yet another heavy raid on Leuna-Merseburg. Only one or two of the rocket fighters got anywhere near the bombers, and none achieved a kill. Against this they lost their own top scorer when Siegfried Schubert's aircraft exploded during take-off,

. . . while 'White 04', winding up to full power (note the shock diamonds in the rocket exhaust), will soon have reached the point of no return – according to German sources, 80 per cent of all Me 163 losses resulted from accidents during take-off or landing!

Safely down, a mottled 'Komet' is retrieved by the Scheuschlepper (a purpose-built lightweight three-wheeled tug towing a tracked trailer), whose two hydraulic arms have lifted the aircraft clear of the ground for transport back to dispersal

as well as Feldwebel 'Nicky' Strassnicky, who was shot down north of Leipzig.

The opening weeks of 1945 saw a bad situation made even worse by a chronic shortage of the Me 163's special fuels. Two further victories were claimed, however. On 16 March Unteroffizier Rudolf Glogner intercepted a reconnaissance Mosquito (which, with one engine on fire, actually managed to make it back to an Allied airfield before crashing). And on the evening of 10 April Leutnant Fritz Kelb, flying an aircraft equipped with the SG 500 '*Jagdfaust*' (literally 'Fighter Fist' – armament consisting of five upward-firing 50 mm rocket-propelled

Aided by a mechanic, a pilot eases himself into the cockpit of his Me 163B. Although wearing the one-piece protective suit and gloves, he has yet to don his oxygen mask. The latter item was worn from the time of take-off not only because of the danger from inhaling toxic hydrogen peroxide fumes if there was the slightest leak in the fuel system, but also as a safeguard in view of the machine's very high rate of climb

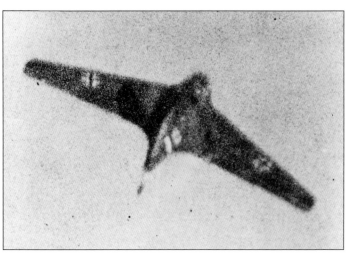

Feldwebel Rudolf Zimmermann's Me 163 is caught on film by the camera-gun fitted to the P-51D of Lt Willard Erkamp during an action fought on 7 October 1944. The 'Komet' pilot was doubly fortunate to be able to crash-land his dam-aged rocket fighter *and* run clear of the machine before it was destroyed on the ground by strafing Mustangs

shells, housed in vertical tubes in each wingroot, which were automatically fired in salvo when actuated by the shadow of an overhead target passing across a light-sensitive cell) brought down one of a force of RAF Lancasters attacking railway yards on the outskirts of Leipzig.

Shortly after this *Stab* and I./JG 400 at Brandis were disbanded. *Kommodore* Wolfgang Späte took his four surviving Me 163 scorers with him to JG 7, where he himself claimed five B-17s in the closing days of the war to finally become a jet ace some three years after first getting involved with the Me 163! Fritz Kelb also downed a B-17, thus emerging as the only pilot to achieve a kill on both the Me 163 and the Me 262, but was himself reported missing five days later on 30 April 1945. The remaining personnel of I./JG 400 were re-mustered as ground troops and despatched southwards to help try to stem the Soviet forces advancing out of Czechoslovakia into Bavaria. The *Gruppe*'s last known 'kill' was a Russian tank destroyed in the border forests by means of a home-made anti-tank gun consisting of a 30 mm MK

Despite the apparent simplicity of the He 162's instrumentation (flying controls grouped on the left and engine gauges on the right), the *Volksjäger* was not an easy machine to master. Note the gunsight mounted above the instruments and the rectangular glazed panel (used as a visual retraction check) in the nosewheel housing ahead of the control column

108 cannon taken from an Me 163 and mounted on a set of jettisonable undercarriage wheels obtained from the same source!

To the north, II./JG 400 retired westwards from Stargard, arriving at Husum in Schleswig-Holstein during the first week of May. Here, Leutnant Peter Gerth claimed a Mosquito, unconfirmed, only hours before the unit surrendered to the British.

It was in the north too, and against the British, that the third and final jet type flown by the Luftwaffe acted out its brief and undistinguished operational career. If the gestation period of the Me 163 had lasted more than half the entire war, then the Heinkel He 162 went to the opposite extreme, progressing from conception, through design and construction, to first flight, all in the space of just 90 days!

Heinkel's brief had been to produce an aircraft that was easy to build, maintain and fly. He may have succeeded in the first two, but the He 162 proved to be anything but easy to fly. It would certainly have been far too much of a handful for the thousands of teenagers of the Hitler Youth earmarked as potential pilots – a proposal had been

Flaps down, an He 162 comes in to land at Leck

put forward by some of the more fanatical of the Third Reich's leaders that an entire year's intake of such youngsters should receive basic glider training before converting directly on to the He 162 to provide a sort of 'aerial *Volkssturm*' (Home Guard). Fortunately for all concerned, this was another scheme overtaken by the course of events, with little ultimately to show for it other than the name commonly bestowed upon the aircraft itself – the '*Volksjäger*', or 'People's Fighter'.

Instead, standard procedure intervened. After the He 162's first flight on 6 December 1944 a service trials unit was set up the following month to evaluate the new design. This was the *Erprobungskommando* 162, based at Rechlin-Roggenthin. But even before the EKdo 162 could complete its work, the first – and only – Luftwaffe combat unit to fly the He 162, Oberstleutnant Herbert Ihlefeld's JG 1, had been withdrawn from the Russian front to begin converting from its Fw 190s on to the new jet.

The next eight weeks, from mid-March until the end of the war, demonstrated what folly it would have been to have entrusted the He 162 to inexperienced youngsters. During this period JG 1 lost nine pilots killed and five wounded in accidents or to unknown causes, and just one to enemy action.

Right
JG 1 COs pose somewhat self-consciously at Leck in May 1945. From left to right, Major Werner Zober (I.*Gruppe*), Oberstleutnant Herbert Ihlefeld (*Geschwaderkommodore*), Hauptmann Heinz Künneke (1.*Staffel*), Oberleutnant Emil Demuth (3.*Staffel*) and Major Bernd Gallowitsch (4.*Staffel*). The next two officers are not members of JG 1, but half-hidden on the far right is Hauptmann Wolfgang Ludewig (2.*Staffel*)

Oberleutnant Emil Demuth, *Staffelkapitän* of 3./JG 1, is pictured beside the tail of his He 162 'White 11' (Wk-Nr 120074 – for marking details see caption to profile number 32) at Leck in May 1945. The 16 victory bars on the tailfin refer to prior kills claimed while flying the Fw 190 with JG 1, the first of these being a B-17 destroyed near Bonn during the Eighth Air Force's historic Schweinfurt-Regensburg mission of 17 August 1943

By 1 May 1945 I. and II./JG 1's He 162s were concentrated just south of the Danish border at Leck, in Schleswig-Holstein. Three days later Leutnant Rudolf Schmitt of 1.*Staffel* made JG 1's sole jet claim – a low-flying RAF Typhoon. It was not allowed, credited instead to a nearby flak unit. And 24 hours after that the first British troops rolled into Leck.

Geographically, little more than 200 kilometres separate Rostock, close to the Baltic coast, from Leck, just inland from the North Sea. But the six eventful years which elapsed between the maiden flight of the Heinkel He 176 in 1939 and the mass surrender of the same company's He 162 '*Volksjäger*' in 1945 had changed the face of aerial warfare for ever.

He 162s of JG 1 drawn up along the perimeter track at Leck after surrender to British forces – note the telltale jeep in the background

APPENDICES

1. The Luftwaffe's Jet Aces

	Total Wartime Victories	Jet Unit(s) Victories	Jet	
Welter, *Oberleutnant* Kurt	63	10./NJG 11	20+	
Bär, *Oberstleutnant* Heinz	220	EJG 2, JV 44	16	
Schall, *Hauptmann* Franz	137	Kdo Now, JG 7	14	KIFA 10/4/45
Buchner, *Oberfeldwebel* Hermann	58	Kdo Now, JG 7	12	
Eder, *Major* Georg-Peter	65	Kdo Now, JG 7	12	W 16/2/45
Rudorffer, *Major* Erich	222	JG 7	12	
Schnörrer, *Leutnant* Karl	46	EKdo 262, Kdo Now, JG 7	11	W 30/3/45
Büttner, *Oberfeldwebel* Erich	8	EKdo 262, Kdo Now, JG 7	8	KIA 20/3/45
Lennartz, *Feldwebel* Helmut	13	EKdo 262, Kdo Now, JG 7	8	
Rademacher, *Leutnant* Rudolf	102	JG 7	8	
Schuck, *Oberleutnant* Walter	206	JG 7	8	
Wegmann, *Oberleutnant* Günther	14	EKdo 262, JG 7	8	W 18/3/45
Weihs, *Leutnant* Hans-Dieter	8	JG 7	8	
Weissenberger, *Major* Theodor	208	JG 7	8	
Ambs, *Leutnant* Alfred	7	JG 7	7	
Arnold, *Oberfeldwebel* Heinz	49	JG 7	7	KIA 17/4/45
Becker, *Feldwebel* Karl-Heinz	7	10./NJG 11	7	
Galland, *Generalleutnant* Adolf	104	JV 44	7	W 26/4/45
Köster, *Unteroffizier* Franz	7	EJG 2, JG 7, JV 44	7	
Müller, *Leutnant* Fritz	22	JG 7	6	
Steinhoff, *Oberst* Johannes	176	JG 7, JV 44	6	W 18/4/45
Baudach, *Oberfeldwebel* Helmut	20	Kdo Now, JG 7	5	KIA 22/2/45
Ehrler, *Major* Heinrich	206	JG 7	5	KIA 6/4/45
Grünberg, *Oberleutnant* Hans	82	JG 7, JV 44	5	
Heim, *Gefreiter* ?	5	JG 7	5	KIA 10/4/45
Neumann, *Leutnant* Klaus	37	JG 7, JV 44	5	
Schreiber, *Leutnant* Alfred	5	Kdo Now, JG 7	5	KIA 26/11/44
Späte, *Major* Wolfgang	99	(JG 400), JG 7	5	

KIA = Killed in action
KIFA = Killed in flying accident
W = Wounded

Approximate Number of Victories by Unit

Erprobungskommando 262	12
Kampfgeschwader 51 'Edelweiss'	8+
Kommando Nowotny	22
III./*Ergänzungsjagdgeschwader* 2	40
Jagdgeschwader 7	500
Kommando Welter (10./NJG 11)	48
Jagdverband 44	55+
Kampfgeschwader (J) 54 'Totenkopf'	50
Kommando Bonow (Ar 234)	0
Jagdgeschwader 400 (Me 163)	10
Jagdgeschwader 1 'Oesau' (He 162)	0
Total (including 10 x Me 163)	**745+**

Luftwaffe Jet Fighter Units – May 1945

LFL.KDO. REICH (NORTHERN SECTOR)

2. Jagddivision (Hackstedt)

I./JG 1	Major Zober	He 162	Leck
7./JG 400	Leutnant Opitz	Me 163	Husum
10./NJG 11	Oberleutnant Welter	Me 262	Schleswig-Jagel

LFL.KDO.6 (SOUTHERN SECTOR)

7. Jagddivision (Saalbach)

JV 44 (IV./JG 7)	Oberstleutnant Bär	Me 262	Salzburg-Maxglan

IX. Fliegerkorps (J) (Radstadt)

Stab JG 7	Major Weissenberger	Me 262	Prague-Ruzyn
I./JG 7	Major Späte	Me 262	Prague-Ruzyn
III./JG 7	Hauptmann Naumann	Me 262	Prague-Ruzyn
Stab KG(J) 6	Oberstleutnant Hogeback	Me 262	Prague-Ruzyn
III./KG(J) 6	Hauptmann Baasner	Me 262	Prague-Ruzyn
I./KG(J) 54	Major Bätcher	Me 262	Prague-Ruzyn
2./KG 51[*]	Hauptmann Abrahamczik	Me 262	Prague-Ruzyn

[*] Fighter-bombers

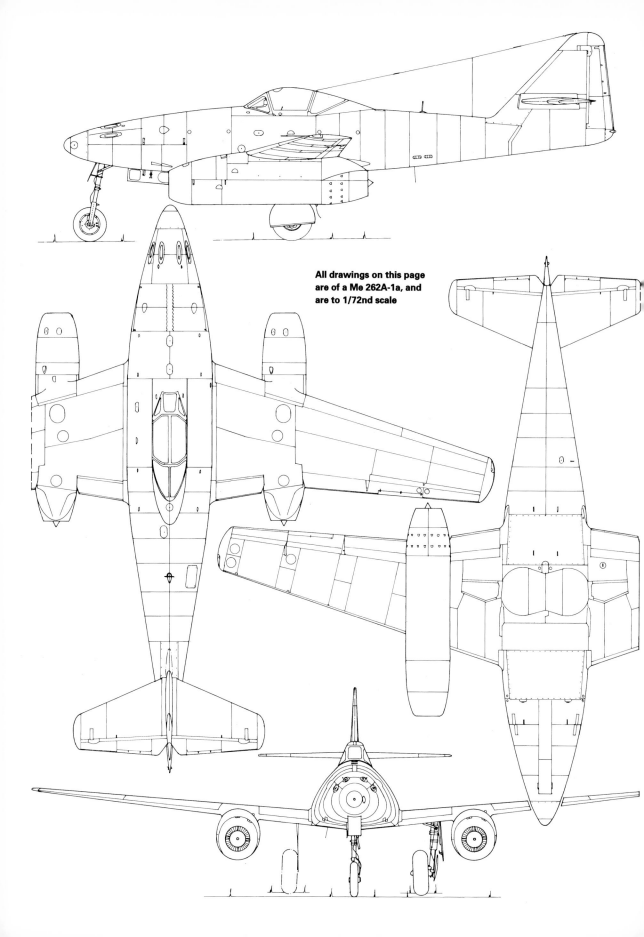

**All drawings on this page
are of a Me 262A-1a, and
are to 1/72nd scale**

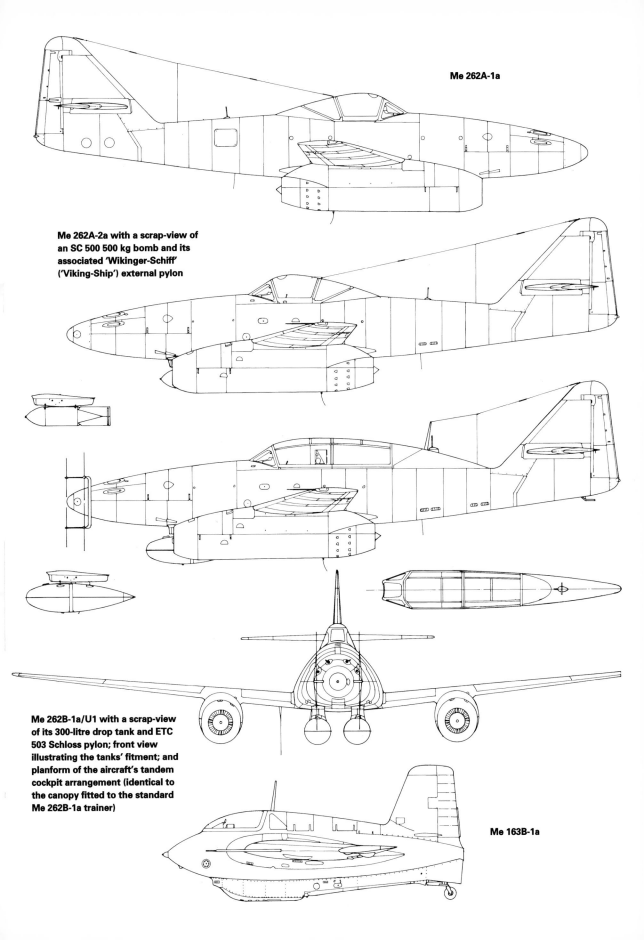

Me 262A-1a

Me 262A-2a with a scrap-view of an SC 500 500 kg bomb and its associated 'Wikinger-Schiff' ('Viking-Ship') external pylon

Me 262B-1a/U1 with a scrap-view of its 300-litre drop tank and ETC 503 Schloss pylon; front view illustrating the tanks' fitment; and planform of the aircraft's tandem cockpit arrangement (identical to the canopy fitted to the standard Me 262B-1a trainer)

Me 163B-1a

COLOUR PLATES

1

Me 262A-1a (Wk-Nr 170063) 'White 9' of Feldwebel Helmut Lennartz, *Erprobungskommando* 262, Rechlin-Lärz, September 1944

Like most early production Me 262s, 'White 9' wears a two-tone grey (74/75) dappled upper finish and pale blue (Weissblau 76) undersides. The mid-fuselage narrow yellow identity band first introduced by EKdo 262 has since caused a certain amount of confusion as, after the unit's disbandment, its aircraft (many still sporting this yellow band) were passed on to other formations including III./EJG 2 and the *Kdo Nowotny*. Lennartz himself, who on 15 August 1944 had claimed the first B-17 to be downed by a Me 262 jet, subsequently went on to serve with both *Kdo Nowotny* and JG 7. He survived the war; having added eight jet kills to the five he had previously scored while flying Bf 109s with II./JG 11.

2

Me 262A-2a '9K+FB' of Leutnant Wilhelm Batel, I./KG 51 'Edelweiss', Saaz (Zatec), May 1945

Unlike the early two-tone grey fighter scheme illustrated above, by war's end the bombers of KG 51 were wearing a variety of camouflage patterns employing, among other shades, dark brown (81) and dark green (82) on the upper surfaces with light or pale blue (65 or 76) undersides; the former often being applied as a dense mottle or scribble. Although the overall finishes of their aircraft may have differed considerably, I./KG 51 were rigorous in maintaining their full four-digit bomber coding (albeit in the late war style, with all but the individual letter reduced in size), plus coloured trim identification – green (as here) for the *Gruppenstab*, and with white, red and yellow denoting 1. to 3. *Staffeln* respectively. Leutnant Batel was one of the very few Me 262 bomber pilots to claim an aerial victory – a P-47 Thunderbolt shot down over Karlsruhe on 16 March 1945.

3

Me 262A-1a (Wk-Nr 110400) 'White 8' of Major Walter Nowotny, *KdoFührer* of the *Kommando Nowotny*, Achmer, November 1944

Although wearing a mid-fuselage yellow band, the distinctive camouflage scheme of 'While 8' – solid fuselage colours coupled with a sharply defined tail mottle – was characteristic of aircraft newly delivered to the short-lived *Kommando Nowotny*. This might suggest that EKdo 262's yellow identity marking was taken over by the *Kdo Nowotny*, who painted their new jets accordingly. Note, too, the yellow cowling ring. 'White 8' was the aircraft in which Russian front veteran, and 258-victory *Experte*, Walter Nowotny flew his one and only jet combat sortie on 8 November 1944 with such tragic results.

4

Me 262A-1a (Wk-Nr 170047) 'White 1' of Leutnant Franz Schall, *Kommando Nowotny*, Hesepe, October 1944

Very similar to the machine depicted above, 'White 1' was the aircraft of Leutnant Franz Schall, Kapitän of the *Kdo Nowotny*'s Hesepe-based *Staffel*. The exact significance of the white 'S' on the rear fuselage is unclear, various sources having suggested that it denotes either the pilot's initial, a

Stab (HQ flight) machine or even a *Schule* (a training aircraft). Schall, another Russian front ace with 123 kills to his credit (with JG 52) prior to joining the *Kdo Nowotny*, claimed a further 14 jet victories before his death on 10 April 1945 when, as *Staffelkapitän* of 10./JG 7, he attempted an emergency landing at Parchim after combat with US fighters, only for his Me 262 to run into a fresh bomb crater and explode.

5

Me 262A-1a (Wk-Nr 110372) 'White 3' of Leutnant Alfred Schreiber, *Kommando Nowotny*, Achmer, November 1944

With its overall dappled finish, Schreiber's 'White 3' is a much more likely candidate to have been an ex-EKdo 262 machine than the two previous profiles. He may even have flown it while himself serving with EKdo 262, during which time he scored his first two confirmed kills (Schreiber had no previous victories to his credit as a *Zerstörer* pilot with ZG 26). He was to claim three more kills while with *Kdo Nowotny*, and thus attain jet ace status, before losing his life in circumstances not dissimilar to Franz Schall. As a member of the newly created 9./JG 7, Schreiber was attempting a single-engined landing at Lechfeld on 26 November 1944 when his wheels caught the lip of a slit trench and his machine cartwheeled.

6

Me 262A-1a (Wk-Nr 110559) 'Red 13' of Oberstleutnant Heinz Bär, *Kommandeur* III./EJG 2, Lechfeld, March 1945

One of the last of a long line of 'lucky thirteens' flown by Heinz Bär during a distinguished and incident-packed wartime career (see *Aircraft of the Aces* volumes 9 and 11 for more details), this aircraft wears an upper surface camouflage combination of dark brown (81) and bright medium green (83) over pale blue (76) undersides. Beginning with a French Curtiss Hawk H-75A shot down on 25 September 1939, Bär had amassed 204 piston-engined aerial victories before transitioning to the Me 262, on which he scored a further 16 to become the leading daylight jet ace, and second only to the nightfighting Kurt Welter in the overall rankings.

7

Me 262C-1a (Wk-Nr. 130186) 'V186' flown by Oberstleutnant Heinz Bär, *Kommandeur* III./EJG 2, Lechfeld, March 1945

At least one of Heinz Bär's 16 jet kills – a P-47 Thunderbolt – was reputedly achieved while flying the prototype 'V186' '*Heimatschützer I*' ('Home Protector I'). This experimental machine had a third engine, a Walter 509A-2 rocket motor, buried in the rear fuselage. Although believed to be finished in similar camouflage colours to 'Red 13' above (albeit in a different pattern), the external differences between the two aircraft are immediately apparent – the most obvious being the 'V186's cutaway lower rudder (to allow for the rocket exhaust), the rocket fuel ventral dump tube and the strengthening band around the rear fuselage at the finroot. After surviving being shot down no fewer than 18 times during the war, Heinz Bär was killed in a light aircraft crash at Brunswick on 28 April 1957.

8

Me 262A-1a (Wk-Nr 170071) 'White 2' of Major Erich

Hohagen, III./EJG 2, Lechfeld, November 1944

Obviously an ex-EKdo 262 machine (note the early camouflage scheme and tell-tale yellow band), 'White 2' was flown by Erich Hohagen both while training with III./EJG 2 and subsequently during his brief tenure of office as the first *Kommandeur* of III./JG 7. One of the *Jagdwaffe*'s 'Old Guard' (his first ten kills had been scored on the Channel front in 1940), Hohagen's tally had risen to 55 by the time he transitioned to the Me 262. But he had also been seriously wounded on a number of occasions, and it was the most recent of these – a severe head injury suffered in the autumn of 1944 – which bedevilled his subsequent combat career with JG 7 and JV 44, and was a contributory factor to his reportedly failing to score a single jet kill.

9

Me 262A-1a 'White 7' of Oberfeldwebel Hermann Buchner, III./EJG 2, Lechfeld, October 1945

Another ex-EKdo 262 candidate, 'White 7' served out its time as a trainer with III./EJG 2. Among those who flew it at Lechfeld was Hermann Buchner, one of the very few to make a successful transition from the ground-attack arm to jet fighters. Having scored 46 aerial victories as a *Schlacht* pilot with SchlG 1 and SG 2 on the Russian front (see *Aircraft of the Aces 6 - Fw 190 Aces of the Russian Front*), he would subsequently claim a dozen heavy bombers while flying the Me 262 with JG 7 – see profile 20.

10

Me 262A-1a (Wk-Nr 170061) 'White 4' of Leutnant Rudolf Harbort, III./EJG 2, February 1945

Having started life as 'White 11' with the *Kdo Nowotny* (note the distinctive sharply-defined mottling of the vertical tail surfaces), in November 1944 Wk-Nr 170061 passed into the hands of III./EJG 2, where it was renumbered 'White 4'. Among those who flew it (in early 1945) was 'Rudi' Harbort, whose four earlier piston-engined kills had left him just short of ace status, a situation he remedied after being posted to JG 7 (where some sources credit him with five jet victories). Meanwhile, 'White 4' ended its days with JV 44 in Austria.

11

Me 262B-1a (Wk-Nr 110494) 'White 9' of Gefreiter Ferdinand Sagemeister, III./EJG 2, Lechfeld, December 1944

Representative of the handful of Me 262 two-seat trainers which reached III./EJG 2 (before production was switched midstream to the interim nightfighter – see profile 21), this rare jet is adorned with an EKdo 262-type mid-fuselage yellow band. Delivered direct to III./EJG 2, this aircraft/marking combination would seem to indicate that the latter unit, too, adopted this marking retroactively. A number of trainee jet pilots had the opportunity to fly 'White 9' during its short-lived career before it crashed, due to a technical fault, south of Augsburg on 12 January 1945, killing the unfortunate Gefreiter Ferdinand Sagemeister.

12

Me 262A-1a (Wk-Nr 111002) 'Green 4' of Major Theodor Weissenberger, *Geschwaderkommodore* JG 7, Brandenburg-Briest, February 1945

This solidly dappled dark brown (81) and medium green (83) machine is typical of JG 7's *Stabskette* aircraft. Being the *Kommodore*'s mount, it bears his horizontal bar markings either side of the fuselage cross, together with a small green '4' below the *Geschwader* badge on the nose. This latter depicts a running fox and was applied in a wide variety of styles, sometimes looking more like a greyhound! Note, too, the blue and red Reich's Defence bands on the rear fuselage. Previously a 200-victory '*Experte*' with JG 5 in the east, Theo Weissenberger claimed a further 8 kills in the Me 262.

13

Me 262A-1a/Jabo (Wk-Nr 111994) 'Green 3' of Hauptmann Erich Mikat, *Geschwaderadjutant* JG 7, Brandenburg-Briest, February 1945

Another *Stabskette* machine, 'Green 3' displays several differences, not only replacing the *Kommodore*'s bars (above) with the single chevron of an adjutant (curiously, a *Gruppen*- rather than *Geschwaderadjutant* marking!), but also sporting a different style of tail swastika. Note, too, the replacement nose cone on an otherwise altogether more freely-applied camouflage scheme, and the two Wgr 21 rocket launcher tubes on the ETC bomb racks under the nose. Like *Kommodore* Weissenberger, Mikat also came to JG 7 from JG 5, but little is known of his career with either unit.

14

Me 262A-1a 'Green 1' of Major Rudolf Sinner, *Gruppenkommandeur* III./JG 7, Brandenburg-Briest, March 1945

Flown by the man who took over from Erich Hohagen (see profile 8) as *Kommandeur* of III./JG 7, Rudi Sinner's Me 262 displays yet a third possible variation of the dark brown (81) and medium green (83) camouflage colours – a hard-edged splinter finish. This is presumably a recently delivered aircraft, for after a while the 'dark' brown faded to an almost purplish green (hence the alternative title of the shade as 'braun-violett'), and would then appear far less sharply defined against the background green 83. Note the *Kommandeur*'s double chevron, and the III.*Gruppe* vertical bar centered on the Reich's Defence bands. This machine also carries a pair of 21 cm rocket launchers. A 37-kill ace who had previously served with JGs 27 and 54, Sinner was seriously wounded when jumped by P-51s while taking off from Rechlin on 4 April 1945.

15

Me 262A-1a (Wk-Nr 500097) 'Yellow 3' of Oberleutnant Hans Waldmann, *Staffelkapitän* 3./JG 7, Kaltenkirchen, March 1945

This slightly more worn and dapple-finished 'Yellow 3' was flown by another ex-Russian front veteran (of JGs 52 and 3), the 132-victory Hans Waldmann. Like so many piston-engined *Experten*, 'Dackel' Waldmann found the Me 262 no easy craft to master, and he had scored just two jet kills before losing his own life in a mid-air collision with his wingman during a bad weather take-off on 18 March 1945. Although Leutnant Hans-Dieter 'Hadi' Weihs landed safely by parachute, Waldmann's body – his chute unopened – was found next day about a kilometre from the crash site of the two aircraft near Schwarzenbek to the east of Hamburg.

16

Me 262A-1a (Wk-Nr 500443) 'Yellow 5' of Unteroffizier Anton Schöppler, 3./JG 7, Saaz, May 1945

A member of Waldmann's *Staffel*, Anton Schöppler had previously served with JG 5, where he had claimed six victories. Some sources credit him with at least the same number again— all US four-engined bombers – during his time with JG 7. Unlike his erstwhile *Staffelkapitän*, Schöppler survived the war, flying his 'Yellow 5' from Saaz (Zatec), in western Bohemia, to Fassberg on the evening of 8 May 1945 to surrender to British forces. His aircraft was later exhibited at Farnborough.

17

Me 262A-1a 'White 15' of Oberfähnrich Rolf Prigge, 4./JG 7, Brandenburg-Briest, February 1945

Rolf Prigge came to JG 7 from IV./JG 27, with whom he had scored just two kills. His aircraft, on the other hand (if the mid-fuselage yellow band is anything to go by), arrived at JG 7 via either the *Kdo Nowotny* or III./EJG 2. Prigge reportedly achieved three victories in February 1945 while flying 'White 15' before, for some unknown reason, being 'RTU'd'.

18

Me 262A-1a 'Red 1' of Leutnant Franz Schall, *Staffelkapitän* 10./JG 7, Parchim, February 1945

Another apparent hand-me-down machine (from III./EJG 2?), Franz Schall's 'Red 1' displays its individual number ahead of the cockpit. Aircraft newly delivered to JG 7 usually had their number applied on the fuselage immediately forward of the Balkenkreuz (see profiles 15 and 16), which was not feasible if the machine was carrying (or had previously carried) a mid-fuselage yellow stripe. It would also appear that machines wearing the yellow stripe did not normally have the blue and red Reich's Defence bands applied, although whether this was a matter of official policy or simply due to a lack of opportunity is not clear. Nor is it known whether 'Red 1' is the aircraft in which Franz Schall met his death (for details see profile 4 notes).

19

Me 262A-1a (Wk-Nr 500491) 'Yellow 7' of Oberfeldwebel Heinz Arnold, 11./JG 7, Prague-Ruzyn, April 1945

In contrast to the above, 'Yellow 7' wears a textbook camouflage finish (81/83/76) and set of markings for an aircraft delivered direct to JG 7. More importantly, it also provides a rare example of a jet pilot's personal scoreboard being displayed on the aircraft itself. Seen immediately aft of the Reich's Defence bands, a horizontal bar topped by the figure 42 indicates the number of piston-engined victories Arnold had scored earlier with JG 5. The seven vertical bars denote his jet kills, claimed within the space of three weeks between 3 and 24 March 1945. When Arnold failed to return from a ground-attack mission in another machine on 17 April 1945, 'Yellow 7' was taken over by Leutnant Fritz Müller. It was he who flew it from Prague-Ruzyn to Lechfeld on 8 May 1945 to surrender. Today, lovingly restored, 'Yellow 7' resides in the US National Air and Space Museum in Washington DC.

20

Me 262A-1a (Wk-Nr 501221) 'Yellow 3' of Oberfeldwebel

Hermann Buchner, III./JG 7, Prague-Ruzyn, April 1945

Fate was far less kind to 'Yellow 7's' sister-ship. 'Yellow 3' was one of a number of aircraft flown by Hermann Buchner, the ex-*Schlacht* pilot (see profile 9 notes), during his period of service with III./JG 7. It was while carrying out a low-level sweep in this machine south of Salzwedel, in Saxony, on 21 April 1945 that Buchner fell foul of US light anti-aircraft fire. After an emergency wheels-up landing, he made good his escape to survive the war with 12 jet kills, all of them four-engined heavy bombers. 'Yellow 3' survived, too, after a fashion, its carcass remaining in the field outside Klötze for many months, a magnet to souvenir-hungry US occupation troops.

21

Me 262B-1a/U1 (Wk-Nr 111980) 'Red 12' of Leutnant Herbert Altner, 10./NJG 11, Reinfeld (nr. Lübeck), May 1945

Typical of the seven interim nightfighters which were delivered to 10./NJG 11 (ex-*Kommando Welter*) during the unit's operational career, Herbert Altner's 'Red 12' wears a two-tone grey (75/76) dapple finish with black undersides and dark green (82) wing and tailplane upper surfaces. Note also the 'Hirschgeweih' ('Stag's Antlers') nose antenna of the FuG 218 Neptun V radar, and the two 300-litre drop tanks on the ETC 503 weapons racks under the nose. Surrendered to the British at Schleswig-Jagel, 'Red 12' subsequently appeared, slightly damaged, at a number of UK postwar static displays and exhibitions, before finally being scrapped after suffering yet further damage during one of the violent storms which buffeted the British Isles in the winter of 1947/48.

22

Me 262A-1a 'White 3' of Generalleutnant Adolf Galland, *Verbandsführer* JV 44, Munich-Riem, April 1945

It is odd that the exact markings of the machine flown by arguably the most famous Me 262 pilot of them all, Adolf Galland, should still give rise to contention. This profile is based upon an illustration checked and amended by the late CO of JV 44 himself. Galland was adamant that his aircraft did not carry a *Kommodore's* horizontal bars (such as seen on Weissenberger's machine – profile 12), but simply wore a 'White 3' in the usual location immediately ahead of the fuselage Balkenkreuz as depicted here. Another source, however (also vetted by Galland), shows the 'White 3' on the forward fuselage (similar to profile 5). In the absence of a mid-fuselage yellow band, this latter marking seems somewhat suspect, but without the support of photographic corroboration, and given the chaotic conditions of the time, plus the numbers of aircraft being handed over to JV 44 from all manner of other units, the questions remain unresolved.

23

Me 262A-1a/U4 (Wk-Nr 111899) of Major Wilhelm Herget, JV 44, Munich-Riem, April 1945

Formerly a Messerschmitt works test vehicle based at Lechfeld, this is the Me 262 armed with the 50 mm Mauser MK 214A nose cannon which 'Willi' Herget brought with him to JV 44 in January 1945. Despite the drabness of the finish and the lack of markings, it would pose quite a challenge to all but the most experienced of modellers; especially if the modified nosewheel (which twisted at right angles on retraction to lie flat beneath the gun) was attempted too. An acknowledged nightfighter *Experte* with 57 victories to his credit (plus 14 by day during earlier *Zerstörer* service), Herget scored just one jet kill – a P-47 on 27 April 1945. Unfortunately, it has been impossible to ascertain whether the Thunderbolt's demise was brought about by use of the temperamental Mauser.

24

Me 262A-1a (Wk-Nr 111745) 'White 5' of Oberfeldwebel Eduard Schallmoser, JV 44, Munich-Riem, April 1945

Another typically drab JV 44 machine with an indeterminate camouflage scheme of faded brown (81) and bright medium green (83) patchily oversprayed by dark green (82), 'White 5' was an early mount of Eduard Schallmoser, wingman to Adolf Galland. It was in this aircraft that Schallmoser opened JV 44's score against the USAAF by ramming a P-38 Lightning near Munich on 3 April 1945. The 'Jet rammer's' career had begun – he would go on to claim a B-26 Marauder and a B-17 Flying Fortress in similar fashion, plus at least one more B-26 by more orthodox means, before the end of the war!

25

Me 262A-1a (Wk-Nr 110556) 'Red S' of Unteroffizier Johann-Karl Müller, JV 44, Brandenburg-Briest, March 1945

One of JV 44's early training hacks, 'Red S' had the scars and dents to prove it. It was flown by a number of newcomers to the unit, including – among others – Johann-Karl Müller who, like Hermann Buchner, was an experienced Russian front Fw 190 *Schlacht* pilot (of II./SG 10). Although he did not enjoy the same sort of success that Buchner achieved with JG 7, 'Jonny' Müller nevertheless later scored at least three jet kills, including two B-26s brought down on 20 April 1945 in a single pass using R4M underwing rockets. Note that the 'Red S' was repeated on the nosewheel door, but the significance of the other stencilling on various fuselage and cowling panels is unknown.

26

Me 262A-1a (Wk-Nr 500042) 'B3+AA' of Oberstleutnant Volprecht Riedesel Freiherr zu Eisenbach, *Geschwaderkommodore* KG(J) 54, Giebelstadt, February 1945

Unlike KG 51, which remained a jet bomber unit throughout, KG 54 was selected to retrain for the fighter role, hence the 'J' (for *Jagd*) in its designation post-September 1944. Initially, however, it retained its four-digit bomber style coding as displayed here on the standard dark brown (81) and bright medium green (83) camouflaged aircraft flown by the *Kommodore*. This machine was one of three total losses (plus three others damaged) suffered in KG(J) 54's first major action against US 'heavies' on 9 February 1945. Hit by return fire from the bombers, B3+AA crashed near Limburg, east of Koblenz, killing Oberstleutnant Riedesel instantly.

27

Me 262A-1a 'B3+white 8' of Hauptmann Werner Tronicke, *Staffelkapitän* 1./KG(J) 54, Zerbst, April 1945

As befitted their new fighter status, KG(J) 54 introduced a revised fuselage code system in the spring of 1945. Although

they kept the 'B3' *Geschwader* designator which had identified their aircraft since the Polish campaign of September 1939, they now did away with the third and fourth letters of the code (denoting the individual aircraft and parent *Staffel*). In their place they used a single fighter-style number, colour coded to indicate the *Staffel*. 'B3+white 8' was one such machine. In it Werner Tronicke downed one B-17 and damaged another on 7 April 1945, before being wounded by return fire and forced to break off the engagement. Pursued by P-51s, he had no option but to take to his parachute, abandoning his damaged aircraft, which crashed near Hagenow.

28

Ar 234B-2 (Wk-Nr 140146) of Hauptmann Kurt Bonow, *KdoFührer* of the *Kommando Bonow*, Oranienburg, March 1945

Based upon a postwar German illustration, this profile offers some indication of the overall finish of the Ar 234 nightfighter. The camouflage scheme, two-tone grey (75/76) dapple over black undersides, is very similar to that of the nocturnal Me 262s (see profile 21). It is believed, however, that in the case of the Arados the dapple extended over the wing and tailplane upper surfaces too. Note that the lower half of the nose glazing has been overpainted black to reduce glare from below. Other points of interest include the nose-mounted radar antennae, the ventral gun pack housing two 20 mm MG 151/20 cannon, and the glazed panel in the roof of the rear fuselage indicating the cramped compartment occupied by Kurt Bonow's rearward facing radar-operator, Oberfeldwebel Beppo Marchetti.

29

Me 163B-0 V41 'PK+QL' of Major Wolfgang Späte, *KdoFührer* of *Erprobungskommando* 16, Bad Zwischenahn, May 1944

This is the aircraft in which Wolfgang Späte flew the world's first operational rocket-fighter sortie on 14 May 1944. Celebrating the culmination of two years' hard work, the groundcrew had given it a special tomato-red paint job overall. Späte was not best pleased when he first caught sight of it, commenting somewhat grumpily that von Richthofen had at least achieved some victories before having his famous triplane painted bright red! On a more practical level, the additional 40 lbs of weight represented by the extra coat of paint would extend the Me 163's notoriously tricky take-off run by a few more unnecessary metres. In the event, it was all to no avail. Späte failed to score on this, or any other occasion that he flew the rocket-fighter. Jet 'acedom' had to wait until his transfer to JG 7 and the Me 262.

30

Me 163B (Wk.-Nr. 163100) 'White 11' of Leutnant Hartmut Ryll, 1./JG 400, Brandis, August 1944

Wearing a much more orthodox finish of standard dark brown (81) and dark green (82) over light blue (76), 'White 11' is the machine in which Hartmut Ryll was shot down on 16 August 1944. Intent on attacking a B-17 straggler, he was bounced by a pair of P-51s and crashed within sight of his Brandis base. After having scored the Me 163's first combat kill a few days earlier, Ryll was also the first member of JG 400 to fall victim to enemy action.

31

Me 163B 'White 9' of Leutnant Fritz Kelb, 1./JG 400, Brandis, January 1945

The pilot of 'White 9', Fritz Kelb, was to score a unique double by claiming a kill in both the Me 163 (a Lancaster on 10 April 1945) *and* the Me 262 (a B-17 on 25 April 1945), although he himself failed to return from a combat mission five days after the latter event. Note the prominent fuel filler point markings for the highly volatile C- and T-Stoff on this machine.

32

He 162A-2 (Wk-Nr 120074) 'White 11' of Oberleutnant Emil Demuth, *Staffelkapitän* 3./JG 1, Leck, May 1945

In a typical He 162 finish of solid dark green upper surfaces and pale blue undersides, Emil Demuth's aircraft displays a wealth of detail. Reading from the front, red, white and black nose rings, plus the red arrowhead common to most 'operational' He 162s. The 'devil-in-the-clouds' badge of I./JG 1 dates back to the *Gruppe*'s Fw 190s, as too does the small '20', which the *Gruppe* used instead of a double chevron to identify a *Kommandeur*'s aircraft (Demuth had served as *Gruppenkommandeur* of I./JG 1 from January to early May 1945). Finally, the 16 victory bars on the tailfin also refer back to successes achieved by Demuth while flying the Fw 190.

33

He 162A-2 (Wk-Nr 120027?) 'White 1' of Leutnant Rudolf Schmitt, 1./JG 1, Leck, May 1945

The sole pilot to claim a victory in the He 162 was Rudolf Schmitt, flying 'White 1' on only his fifth combat mission. But his claim – for the destruction of an RAF Typhoon on 4 May 1945 – was not allowed, being credited instead to a local flak unit. Note the variations in 'White 1's' camouflage and markings from the previous profile – the higher demarcation line between upper and lower surfaces, the altered style of national insignia, lack of nose rings (and slightly amended arrowhead), relocation of individual numeral and the completely different badge. The latter, very similar to that of Stab KG 30, is believed to indicate 1.*Staffel*.

FIGURE PLATES

1

Major Georg-Peter Eder, *Staffelkapitän* of 9./JG 7 at Parchim in February 1945, is seen wearing typical late-war garb of a two-piece black leather zippered flying suit with large patch pockets on each thigh, plus officer's pattern belt and the Luftwaffe version of the M1943 'standard model' soft cap issued to all services. Note also the sun-goggles, rank tabs, and the Knight's Cross with Oak Leaves at his throat. Scoring his first two kills on 22 June 1941 (the opening day of the attack on the Soviet Union), Eder's incident-packed career included being shot down on 17 occasions and wounded a dozen times in the process!

2

Generalleutnant Adolf Galland, *Kommandeur* of JV 44 at Munich-Riem in April 1945. Sartorially – as well as operationally – independent as ever, the ex-*General der Jagdflieger* opts for a pair of zippered, lined, leather trousers (without pockets), plus one of his favourite fur-collared grey leather jackets. During his periods of service at the front, Galland wore a wide range of non-regulation clothing, including several examples of captured enemy equipment. But two items remained constant throughout – the battered 'campaign' cap, here resplendent in General's gold trim, and the ever present cigar.

3

Leutnant Karl 'Quax' Schnörrer of JG 7, based at Munich-Riem in March 1945, was a long-time wingman and personal friend of Walter Nowotny in Russia, and had subsequently served in the latter's jet *Kommando*. Here, Schnörrer wears a leather flying jacket with zip pockets and regulation uniform trousers. Note the lightweight 'Netzkopf' flying helmet and sun goggles, and the rank tabs and Knight's Cross awarded on 22 March 1945. All but two of the eleven victories he claimed while flying the Me 262 were four-engined bombers.

4

Oberleutnant Kurt Welter was *Staffelkapitän* of 10./NJG 11 (*Kommando Welter*), based at Burg, near Magdeburg, in April 1945. He is seen wearing yet another variation of the ubiquitous black leather flying jacket, worn with breeches and standard flying boots, for the highest-ranking jet ace of them all. Welter received the Oak Leaves to his Knight's Cross on 18 March 1945. Note, too, the privately purchased sunglasses – not an affectation, but used by many nightfighters to accustom their eyes to darkness. Having survived the war, Welter was killed in a freak accident four years later, on 7 March 1949, when his car, waiting at a level-crossing near Leck (last stop for JG 1's He 162s), was crushed by logs falling from an improperly loaded passing train.

5

Major Wolfgang Späte, *Geschwaderkommodore* of JG 400 at Brandis in April 1945, models the special one-piece suit designed to protect pilots flying the Me 163. Note the elasticated cuffs to the gloves and boot tops. The goggles and oxygen mask were essential extras to guard against toxic vapour fumes in the cockpit. Although it was claimed to be acid-proof by the manufacturers, many pilots complained that the material of the suit 'leaked like a sieve'. Späte failed to score in the Me 163, but subsequently achieved last-minute jet 'acedom' on the Me 262.

6

Hauptmann Franz Schall, *Staffelkapitän* of 10./JG 7 at Parchim in March 1945, wears breeches similar to those worn by Kurt Welter, but paired with knee boots and a lightweight flying blouse. Prominent are the Luftwaffe eagle on the right breast, hauptmann's rank tabs on the shoulders, and the Knight's Cross, which had been awarded on 10 October 1944 for 177 victories. After transferring to jets, first with the *Kommando Nowotny* and then JG 7, Schall scored 14 kills before he lost his own life on 10 April 1945 during an emergency landing at Parchim when his Me 262 ran into a bomb crater and exploded.